THE STRUGGLE FOR AN ENLIGHTENED REPUBLIC:

BUENOS AIRES AND RIVADAVIA

The Struggle for an Enlightened Republic:

Buenos Aires and Rivadavia

Klaus Gallo

British Library Cataloguing-in-Publication Data
A catalogue record for this book is available
from the British Library

ISBN   1 900039 76 1   1005633910

INSTITUTE FOR THE STUDY OF THE
A M E R I C A S
UNIVERSITY OF LONDON · SCHOOL OF ADVANCED STUDY

Institute for the Study of the Americas
Senate House
Malet Street
London WC1E 7HU
Telephone: 020 7862 8870
Fax: 020 7862 8886
Email: americas@sas.ac.uk
Web: americas.sas.ac.uk

CONTENTS

Introduction

Bernardino Rivadavia is mostly remembered in Argentina for having been the first president in the history of the nation. The fact that the presidential chair is still to this day referred to as '*el sillón de Rivadavia*' corroborates this. Rivadavia is perceived by many as a historic figure identified with liberalism, in the term's loose association with free trade, and, very much in connection with this concept, as a politician who sustained close commercial and political ties with Great Britain. This vision of Rivadavia is by no means exaggerated; however, it reveals a rather limited and schematic idea of the character's political and ideological profile.

The fact that Rivadavia is most frequently associated with Argentina's first presidency is of interest since it was not precisely for this reason that he proved to be one of the most acclaimed and, at the same time, controversial personalities of the new nation. His office lasted only a year and a half of the four years stipulated by the 1826 Constitution, and he was forced to resign in mid-1827 due to the complicated local and foreign political scenario of the River Plate provinces, as they were then referred to. Only a few Argentines now associate him with the government of Buenos Aires headed by General Martín Rodríguez, *la feliz experiencia* as it was labelled by its contemporaries (literally 'the happy experience'), in which Rivadavia acted as *Ministro de Gobierno*, a post similar to that of prime minister, from 1821–24, displaying the political skills that helped transform him into a *prócer* (a national hero) of the first stages of Argentina's national existence.

With respect to Rivadavia's ideological inclinations, one frequently hears him referred to as a *liberal pro-inglés*, an attribution that owes much to his alleged devotion to free trade, but more significantly to the loan Argentina contracted with Baring Brothers in 1822, which he did much to facilitate.

His strong attraction to the principles of utilitarianism is, however, seldom mentioned in the general histories of Argentina. This

English school of thought proclaimed the necessity of establishing laws that would provide wider levels of happiness to a larger number, a goal that implied the adoption of democratic principles under a republican form of government. Rivadavia did not show much inclination towards the pro-monarchic and aristocratic features of the 'classical liberal tradition' encapsulated in certain philosophic currents of thought of the late eighteenth and early nineteenth century such as the Scottish School of Enlightenment. These distinctions enable one to assess more accurately the type of 'liberal model' Rivadavia was to be guided by during most of his political career.

Rivadavia was connected in many ways to Britain, as can be perceived by his affiliation with utilitarianism and by his many acquaintances who were inhabitants of that nation, especially entrepreneurs and diplomats. His obsession, while he was acting as minister of the Buenos Aires government, with achieving the British government's recognition of Argentine independence further explains why many local historians have emphasised this link. However, it is important to point out that Rivadavia was equally attached to issues and ideological trends from other European countries, especially France. His association with certain politicians, diplomats and philosophers, especially those connected with the Ideology school of thought, is clear evidence of his equally significant relation with that nation. The theoretical propositions of the so-called *idéologues* were similar to those of the utilitarians in Britain, and they essentially favoured the re-establishment of republicanism in their country but under a more moderate version than during the French Revolution. One could say that the reforms put forward by Rivadavia and his government during the *feliz experiencia* were an attempt to introduce order, without renouncing republicanism, after the continual political upheavals that took place during the first decade of Argentina's independent existence.

This book is not a biography of Rivadavia. Neither does it seek to analyse the very controversial economic circumstances that led to his presidency's eventual downfall in 1827. It is, however, a work concerned with the powerful influence exercised by this character in Argentina, most specifically with respect to the political and cultural project that he and his group of followers attempted to promote during the *feliz experiencia* of the 1820s in Buenos Aires. The main focus of analysis will be on *porteño* society (*porteños* are the inhabitants of the city) and on the effects the Rodríguez government reforms had on it. It is, therefore, a survey that covers a significant segment of Rivadavia's political life, but by no means its totality.

The opening chapter centres on the forging of Rivadavia's political career during the early stages of the independence process in Argentina. A turning point of his career was the diplomatic mission he was entrusted with by the *Directorio* government in 1814, which allowed Rivadavia to spend almost six years residing in Europe, mostly in Britain and France. At a time when the Congress of Vienna was attempting to re-impose authoritarian monarchic governments after the traumatic effects of the Napoleonic period, Rivadavia became acquainted with European republicans such as Jeremy Bentham and Destutt de Tracy, who would have a most significant influence on the shaping of the Argentine's political ideas.

Chapter 2 assesses the implications of Benthamite and utilitarian influences during the reform period of the *feliz experiencia*, and in what ways Rivadavia and his group were responsible for introducing a series of measures in political, religious and cultural spheres. These clearly manifested the radical direction formulated by his government, especially if one compares them with the mainstream liberal tendencies of the early nineteenth century. It had become apparent that the political elite of Buenos Aires was more inclined towards applying so-called 'laws of utility' than the natural law tradition that had prevailed amongst previous River Plate political actors throughout the first decade of independence. The adoption of this approach was deemed necessary in order to rectify political and cultural practices.

The attempts of the Rodríguez government to bring about a process of political and cultural regeneration, by enhancing the scope of public opinion as well as encouraging the organisation of civic festivities and theatrical representations more in line with the trends already prevalent in the European stages, will be analysed in Chapter 3. The Rivadavian publicists attempted to promote the government's reform programme by increasing the number of newspapers published in order to inform a wider public. Publishing extracts of the works of Enlightenment authors in newspapers for the purpose of gaining support for ecclesiastical reform is an example of these efforts, as are the articles that stressed the necessity for *porteño* society to come to terms with more 'modern' forms of cultural representations in order to eradicate the archaic remnants of Spanish customs and values. This attempt to bring about such an ambitious cultural transformation would eventually generate a climate of increasing social tensions reflected in the serious political antagonisms that arose in the River Plate in the late 1820s.

Chapter 4 covers the last years of the Rivadavian era culminating with the unsuccessful presidential experience. The particularity of this last section resides in the fact that it consists of a series of contrasting accounts by British observers during the years of Rivadavia's hold on *rioplatense* (River Plate) politics, almost resembling a 'rise and fall' narrative of that process. Such an approach reveals the nuances of Rivadavia's dealings with Britain and her subjects. The high level of praise directed towards Rivadavia by British diplomats and commercial agents at the time of the *feliz experiencia* mutated into deception and criticism during the period he was president.

This work is based on a series of three lectures I delivered at the Institute of Latin American Studies of the University of London (ILAS) during the months of January and February of 2004, whilst I was Visiting Fellow there. I am very grateful to the ILAS Director James Dunkerley for his extreme generosity and kindness throughout my stay, and for providing me with the opportunity to discuss aspects of my research in these presentations with colleagues I much admire and esteem. I am also indebted to him for encouraging me to publish this book. My thanks are also due to Olga Jiménez, Alison Underhill, Eugenia Borrajo Serra, Karen Perkins and the rest of the secretarial and academic staff of the Institute.

1

The Making of a *Rioplatense* Politician

Bernardino de la Trinidad González Rivadavia was born in Buenos Aires on 20 May 1780. His father, Bernardino Benito González Rivadavia, arrived in the River Plate from his native Galicia in Spain and became a famous lawyer, acting at one point in the *Real Audiencia*. His mother, Josefa de Jesús Rodríguez y Ribadeneira, also of Galician descent, was born in Buenos Aires. Bernardino Rivadavia was the third of the couple's five children.[1]

In 1798, Rivadavia was admitted to the prestigious Colegio de San Carlos in Buenos Aires, where he studied philosophy and theology. In 1803 he decided to abandon his studies apparently to assist his father with his business. When the British invasions of the River Plate took place in 1806–07, Rivadavia enrolled in a militia unit formed by descendants of Galicians and, according to certain accounts, was active in the final battles of the epic *Reconquista* of Buenos Aires, where the combined Spanish and Creole forces eventually defeated the British in July 1807.

Shortly after these momentous events Rivadavia was designated *Alférez Real* by the Viceroy and hero of the British invasions Santiago de Liniers, who had been closely acquainted with Rivadavia's family in the past. This was an office of the greatest honour in the *cabildo* (the town council) as it involved custody and public bearing of the royal banner and substituting for the *alcalde* (the local magistrate) if he were absent. In 1809, Rivadavia married Juana del Pino, the daughter of Joaquín del Pino, who had acted as Viceroy — the most important administrative and political position in the Spanish

---

1   R. Piccirilli, *Rivadavia y su tiempo* (2 vols., Buenos Aires, 1943) remains to this day the standard biography on Rivadavia. Also worth mentioning are A. Palcos, *Rivadavia: Ejecutor del pensamiento de Mayo* (La Plata, 1960) and C.S.A. Segreti, *Bernardino Rivadavia: Hombre de Buenos Aires, ciudadano argentino* (Buenos Aires, 1999).

Colonial Empire — of the United Provinces of the River Plate between 1801 and 1804.

By the time of his marriage the political situation in the River Plate provinces, which had been notable for its stability since the creation of the Viceroyalty in 1776, had become increasingly tense thanks to the Spanish crown's delicate situation following the Napoleonic invasions of the Iberian Peninsula. Matters got worse for the Viceroy of the River Plate provinces, Baltasar Cisneros, when news announcing the fall of the Junta of Seville reached Buenos Aires in May 1810. This information precipitated the decision of the local authorities to convene a *cabildo abierto*, an open town council, where Creoles and Spaniards would deliberate on the future course of action to adopt.

Rivadavia participated in the *cabildo abierto* of 22 May and, like most of the Creoles participating in this event, voted in favour of declaring independence from Spain, under the pretext that if that nation was ruled by a foreign usurper of the throne, sovereignty in the colonies should temporarily revert to a government formed by local people. He did not, however, join the first autonomous River Plate government, the *Primera Junta*, which came into existence on 25 May after the Creoles forced Cisneros to resign as Viceroy and after they declared independence from the Spanish Empire for as long as the French remained in power in Spain, swearing allegiance to the future Ferdinand VII, son of the deposed Charles IV. Shortly after that declaration was approved, tensions broke out within the new government as a result of the emergence of two rival tendencies: on the one hand a more conservative faction, led by the junta's president Cornelio Saavedra, that seemed determined to comply with the partial declaration of independence, and on the other, the faction headed by Mariano Moreno, the junta's secretary, a lawyer attached to Rousseaunian ideals who ordered translated extracts of *The Social Contract* to be published in *La Gazeta*, the official newspaper established by the new independent government, and visibly inclined towards radicalising the revolutionary process.[2]

2   T. Halperín Donghi, *Revolución y guerra: Formación de una élite dirigente en la Argentina criolla* (Buenos Aires, 1972) and *Historia argentina: De la revolución de independencia a la Confederación Rosista* (Buenos Aires, 1972), along with the more recent contribution of J.C. Chiaramonte, *Ciudades, provincias, estados: Orígenes de*

Most historians believe that Rivadavia favoured the Morenistas, despite the fact that they were led by a man with whom he had not been on good terms in the past. His support for that faction seemed to be confirmed when the *Junta* ordered Rivadavia's confinement to the locality of Salto, alleging his '*positiva oposición a nuestro sistema de gobierno*' after open confrontation between the Saavedrista and Morenista factions in April of the following year. These events took place shortly after Moreno's tragic death early in 1811, when a group of Saavedra's supporters instigated a revolt in order to oust the Morenistas who remained inside the government. It was at this juncture that a new *Junta de Seguridad*, a repressive government organ created for the purpose of persecuting the junta's enemies, exiled Rivadavia and others who were suspected of conspiring against the government. The *Junta de Seguridad* declared, however, that they had exiled Rivadavia on account of his family ties with Juan Michelena, a Spanish officer married to one of his sisters and who was collaborating with the Spanish resistance in Uruguay, which seems to be an absolutely ungrounded accusation.[3]

The *Junta de Seguridad* was not to last much longer in power. Shortly after hearing the news of the Argentine army's defeat in the Alto Perú against the Spanish forces in mid-1811, the *cabildo* of Buenos Aires, which preserved its colonial institutional framework by still acting as a kind of town council or superintendence in the first years after independence, declared the suppression of the *Junta* as an executive body, subsequently transforming it into a legislative body called the *Junta de Observación*, and the establishment of a new government, later referred to as the *Primer Triunvirato*, which took over in September of the same year. This governmental change, the first of many in Argentina's extremely tumultuous first decade of independent existence, entailed the elevation of Rivadavia to the upper ranks of the incipient political system in the River Plate.

The designation of the three members of the new government — Juan José Paso, Manuel de Sarratea and Feliciano Chiclana —

---

la nación argentina (1800–1846) (Buenos Aires, 1997), are three of the most comprehensive general studies on the first stages of the independence period in Argentina.

3 Piccirilli, *Rivadavia y su tiempo*, vol. 2, p. 126.

resulted from elections held within the members of the *Cabildo*, where Rivadavia obtained 360 votes, which proved enough for him to become the new secretary of the *Triunvirato*. During the year-long existence of the *Primer Triunvirato*, Rivadavia was increasingly looked upon as one of its most prominent members, and he ended up being designated a *Triunviro* himself. His first experience in office was marred by the continuing political upheavals, but Rivadavia did earn a moderate degree of support during his first months in power after he promulgated a series of progressive measures. Amongst these were the *Triunvirato*'s decree that considerably liberalised commerce for both local and foreign investors, a decree that widened freedom of expression and the law by which the slave trade was abolished. Rivadavia was also thought to be responsible for a series of initiatives applied in the cultural sphere, including the creation of a museum of natural history, the development of institutions of secondary level education and the creation of a public library and a national archive.

However, other reforms dictated by the government generated an atmosphere of increasing tension and instability in the River Plate region. The controversial *Estatuto Provisional*, which according to most accounts was inspired by Rivadavia, suppressed the *Junta de Observación* as a legislative body until a new national legislative assembly was formed, putting more power in the hands of the *Triunvirato*. The political controversies that arose as a consequence of this document provoked much political confusion — Tulio Halperín sarcastically criticises the *Estatuto* for its '*extrema vaguedad*' — as it only served to increase the levels of antagonism between the rival political factions in Buenos Aires, and also between the government and representatives of the provinces, who were irritated by its undisguised centralism. His membership of the *Triunvirato* meant that Rivadavia was continually accused by his opponents for being a promoter and typical exponent of the so-called *centralismo porteño*, an accusation that was to remain for the rest of his political career.[4]

The most visible focus of opposition in Buenos Aires at that time was the Morenista political group that operated under the name of *Sociedad Patriótica* — an excellent imitation of a French revolutionary

4   Halperín Donghi, *Historia argentina*, p. 90.

club according to Halperín — led by Bernardo de Monteagudo, an exile from the Alto Perú, who rapidly became one of the most influential radical publicists in the River Plate during the first decade of independence, editing *La Gazeta* for a few years.[5] The *Sociedad Patriótica* was increasingly critical of the *Triunvirato's* lack of initiatives and resolution to establish an independent state, and also of its ambivalence towards the situation in Uruguay. The government's inability to deal with the complicated political situation in that region was openly evident. The successful resistance of the Spanish forces in Montevideo and the gradual penetration of Portuguese troops from the north into the Banda Oriental, as well as the widespread popularity of the Uruguayan *caudillo* Gervasio de Artigas, who had already distanced himself from the River Plate authorities, proved too much to handle for the *Triunvirato* government.

Another source of problems for Rivadavia lay in the military sphere. In December 1811, members of the *Patricios* Regiment, one of the most popular urban militia divisions, created during the British invasions, attempted a rebellion against Manuel Belgrano, the new commander designated by the *Triunvirato*, who tried to impose a new disciplinary regime. Further complications arose in mid-1812, when Creole officers who had fought for the Spanish armies in the Peninsular War against the French, such as Carlos María de Alvear and José de San Martín (both of them members of the recently formed *Logia Lautaro*, a South American military lodge) arrived in Buenos Aires and almost immediately established close connections with the *Sociedad Patriótica*. These two groups became increasingly impatient with what they viewed as an excessively timid management of the independence process by the *Triunvirato*. After receiving news of the Royalist defeat in Tucumán by the patriot forces, they decided to stage a rebellion, which eventually forced the government's dissolution in October 1812. The combination of opposition forces composed of local radical activists and prestigious military officers just returned from Spain, plus the substantial support from important sectors of the army, proved decisive in forcing this political takeover.

5   *Ibid.*, p. 91.

For the next 18 months Rivadavia decided to stay away from political life. During this period, a second *Triunvirato* was set up and a constituent assembly, containing representatives from all the provinces, was convened to establish a new legislative body and a constitution with the clear intention of decreeing a definite separation from the Spanish monarchy. In spite of achieving significant advances in terms of the latter objective — declaration of popular sovereignty, replacement of the royal seal by a patriotic design, adoption of national flag and anthem — the members of the Assembly of the Year XIII, as it was later referred to, did not succeed in writing a new constitution or in providing a more stable and credible political system.

The lack of resolution of the Assembly has been mainly attributed to the increasingly complex regional and international context. On the one hand, the situation in Uruguay was far from being resolved; on the other, the news of the liberation of Spain, and so the imminent arrival on the throne of Ferdinand VII, provoked high levels of anxiety and uncertainty in the River Plate. The prospect of establishing a more dynamic and independent itinerary was now treated with much scepticism within the *rioplatense* political elite. Furthermore, the fact that Great Britain had been so instrumental in the success of the Peninsular War left only a small margin of hope that it would be willing to extend formal recognition of the River Plate provinces as a sovereign nation. This had been a major diplomatic objective since independence had been declared.

It was precisely the need to secure Great Britain's attention, despite the fact that she had now established a solid alliance with Spain, which motivated the *Segundo Triunvirato* to send Manuel de Sarratea as diplomatic agent to England and France. Towards the end of 1813 this government was replaced by the *Directorio*, which reinforced the diplomatic venture by sending both Manuel Belgrano and Rivadavia to Europe.

A Voyage of Diplomacy and Ideological Discovery

The two men were commissioned by Gervasio Posadas, the first Supreme Director of the United Provinces of the River Plate, at the beginning of 1814 to fulfil this diplomatic task. Belgrano, one of the leading figures of the political and military scene since independence had been declared, would eventually remain in Europe for much less time than Rivadavia. The main aim of this mission consisted in seeking formal recognition from Spain and other European courts, most especially Britain and France, of Argentina's partially declared independence. The most conspicuous instigator behind this project was General Alvear, who was Posadas's nephew and had gained a visible degree of popularity since returning to the River Plate thanks mainly to his successful scheming inside the *Logia Lautaro* and the *Sociedad Patriótica*, which enabled him to become a key political actor. His military talents — evidenced throughout the wars of independence and later in the mid-1820s, when the war with the Brazilian Empire broke out — undoubtedly helped enhance his reputation.

Alvear eventually became *Director Supremo* in 1815 and, like his predecessors in power, was rapidly overcome by the political tensions in the region, largely caused by the interior provinces' increasing grievances over the centralism sought by the Buenos Aires–based *rioplatense* governments. At the same time, he also had to confront the permanent threat of a takeover in Uruguay by Portuguese troops, given the relentless attempts of the Empire to control that region. These concerns were dramatically revealed when Alvear sent a diplomatic envoy to make secret contact with British delegates attached to the Portuguese court in Rio de Janeiro, hoping to obtain their assistance in alleviating the chaotic political situation in the Platine provinces. This highly controversial endeavour finally came to nothing. The main passage of his letter to the British authorities in Rio gives some idea of the state of desperation he was in at that moment:

> These provinces desire to become part of Great Britain, obey their Government and live under their powerful influence. They submit themselves without any type of condition to the generosity and good faith of the English nation, and I am resolved to sustain such a just cause to liberate her from the evils that afflict her.[6]

6   'Estas provincias [United Provinces of the River Plate] desean pertenecer a la Gran Bretaña, obedecer su gobierno y vivir bajo su influjo poderoso. Ellas se abandonan sin condición alguna a la generosidad y buena fé del pueblo inglés, y yo estoy resuelto a sostener tan justa solicitud para librarla de los males que la afligen.'

The particular timing of the Belgrano–Rivadavia mission to Europe turned out to be unfortunate. In the midst of Bonaparte's collapse and the subsequent emergence of the ultra-conservative Congress of Vienna and the Holy Alliance, which were deeply suspicious of South American republics fighting for their independence from Spain, the chances of this diplomatic venture receiving sympathetic responses seemed remote.[7] Partly as a result of the traumatic legacy that both the French revolutionary cycle and Bonaparte's Empire represented for Europe, the continental bodies were unwilling to formally accept the emancipation of the former Spanish colonies in America, essentially because of the obsession of the powers which composed the so-called Congress System with fully re-establishing monarchical rule throughout Europe. The fact that most of the new South American states had adopted republican systems of government, and expressed no desire whatsoever to return to their former colonial status once Ferdinand VII was returned to the Spanish throne, partially explains the reluctance of these diplomatic organs to recognise or provide assistance of any sort to them.[8]

In view of these circumstances, the prospects of success for the Belgrano–Rivadavia mission were slim. Both diplomatic agents, after receiving instructions from the Supreme Directors of the River Plate — first Carlos María de Alvear and, from 1816, Juan Martín de Pueyrredón — sought to secure the necessary means for establishing a monarchic government in those provinces. It was now assumed by most of the *rioplatense* political actors that the creation of a constitutional monarchy would increase the credibility of the River Plate and

---

Manuel García, Alvear's special envoy to Brazil, decided not to deliver this letter to the British authorities. As legend has it, the person who apparently dissuaded García from obeying his orders was none other than Rivadavia, who was at that time in Rio awaiting to sail for his mission in Europe. B. Mitre, *Historia de Belgrano* (Buenos Aires, 1887), vol. III, p. 347.

7   The bulk of the correspondence between Rivadavia and his government during this mission can be found in Universidad de Buenos Aires, *Comisión de Bernardino Rivadavia ante España y otras potencias de Europa 1814–1820* (2 vols., Buenos Aires, 1933–36).

8   W.W. Kaufmann, *British Policy and the Independence of Latin America 1804–1828* (New Haven, 1951), pp. 81–93.

enhance the chances of recognition by European nations. When, for instance, Belgrano returned to the River Plate in 1816, he began to promote a most peculiar monarchical project that consisted of establishing a descendant of the Inca on a *rioplatense* throne. His exotic proposal was debated and dismissed at the Congress of Tucumán, where in July 1816 Argentina's complete independence was finally declared.[9]

For most of the rest of his stay in Europe, Rivadavia was to find himself engulfed in a series of ill-conceived monarchical schemes, most of which were instigated by Sarratea, who was still acting as the River Plate's diplomatic envoy in Europe where he had since 1814 been dealing with obscure European agents in a quest to 'find' a prince with suitable credentials to occupy an eventual *rioplatense* crown. The excessive hope the *Directorio* seems to have placed on this monarchic enterprise reflected the uncertain political situation that prevailed even after the declaration of full independence; it also partly explains the efforts of that government to comply with the Congress of Vienna's criteria of legitimate and acceptable models of government.

In 1819, during Pueyrredón's administration, a plan to install a French monarch in the River Plate was seriously considered both in Buenos Aires and in France. Pueyrredón, who was of French ancestry, wrote to the Duc de Richelieu, one of Louis XVIII's most influential ministers, in March 1818 offering to establish formal commercial relations. Although his letter was never answered, the arrival in the River Plate a few months later of Hilaire Lemoyne, an emissary of the French crown, gave the Supreme Director a chance to re-establish connections with France. It was this agent who later suggested that Louis Philippe Duc d'Orléans, future king of France, was the ideal candidate for the local throne, an idea that Pueyrredón favoured.[10]

When Lemoyne returned to France, Pueyrredón decided to send José Valentín Gómez, a canon of the cathedral of Buenos Aires and former teacher of Rivadavia at the Colegio de San Carlos, on a secret mission to Paris to advance the matter. In mid-1819 Gómez met the French foreign minister, the Marquis Dessolles, who had already

9   K. Gallo, *Great Britain and Argentina: from Invasion to Recognition 1806–1826* (Houndmills, 2001), pp. 118–19.
10   *Ibid.*, p. 125.

been informed of the situation in the River Plate by Rivadavia, and who now seemed to fancy the idea of establishing a monarchy there. However, the French foreign minister advised Gómez that it would be more convenient to nominate a candidate other than Orléans; someone connected to both the French and the Spanish royal families. He suggested the Duke of Lucca, son of a sister of Ferdinand VII and King Louis of Parma. This candidate, however, was not considered sufficiently distinguished by Gómez, who in turn decided to delay his response until he received further orders from home. In spite of her persistence, France had to abandon the whole project once Spain and the other European nations found out about the secret negotiations, becoming further enraged when the French government refused to offer any sort of explanation.[11]

News of these machinations produced an outburst of fury within British public opinion. *The Times* strongly criticised the secret monarchical schemes of the French in the River Plate, blaming the Tory administration of Lord Liverpool for not acting more resolutely in this matter and claiming that the cabinet had 'always treated the South Americans with the greatest reserve, as if fearing contamination by simple contact'. The newspaper reckoned that 'British interest is likely to gain the ascendancy in the River Plate, rather through the disposition of the inhabitants than any influence exerted by our ministers'.[12] These remarks came from a newspaper that had originally supported the Liverpool administration's line of conduct towards Spanish American affairs.[13]

In spite of these complicated and stressful diplomatic misfortunes, other aspects of Rivadavia's European trip would turn out more positively for the *rioplatense* agent, particularly those which exercised a tangible effect on his intellectual formation and later inspired the shaping of the governmental project he would attempt upon his return to Buenos Aires a few years later. Almost six years of resi-

---

11   W.S. Robertson, *France and Latin American Independence* (Baltimore, 1939), pp. 157–76; M. Belgrano, *La Francia y la monarquía en el Plata* (Buenos Aires, 1933), p. 69.
12   *The Times*, 3 July 1820.
13   Gallo, *Great Britain and Argentina*, pp. 127–9.

dence in Europe allowed Rivadavia to witness the political scene in countries like Britain and France at first hand, and they also enabled him to make the acquaintances of influential political thinkers of both countries, such as the utilitarians Jeremy Bentham and James Mill in Britain, and the *idéologues* Destutt de Tracy and Pierre Daunou in France, who supported the cause of the Spanish American colonies and were instrumental in upholding basic republican ideals at a time when they seemed to be slipping away from Rivadavia's clutches.

Rivadavia and the Political-intellectual Scene in Britain and France

The socio-economic situation in Britain after the conclusion of the Napoleonic Wars in 1815 was complex in many respects. Even though the Tory government of Lord Liverpool, prime minister since 1812, had strengthened its power and popular support thanks to the decisive role it displayed during the last stages of the Napoleonic Wars, the economic problems that arose in Great Britain precisely as a consequence of that European conflict contributed to a volatile social situation, particularly between 1816 and 1820.[14] A series of popular protests organised by groups of workers and artisans took place during the years Rivadavia resided in the country, and were essentially a result of increasing unemployment levels and low salaries, the Spa Fields riots of 1816 and the Peterloo Massacres of 1819 probably being the most dramatic of these instances. The latter, which took place at St. Peter's Fields, near Manchester, ended in serious turmoil with 11 people killed and many injured as a consequence of the military intervention ordered by the government, which had also suspended habeas corpus.[15]

On the other hand, the foreign policy of the Liverpool administration tended to favour the conservative principles fostered by the Congress of Vienna. This approach was clearly evident in the decisive role played by the British foreign minister, Lord Castlereagh,

---

14 F. Crouzet, 'The Impact of the French Wars on the British Economy,' in H.T. Dickinson (ed.), *Britain and the French Revolution 1789–1815* (London, 1989), pp. 189–209.

15 In relation to this episode, E.P. Thompson, *The Making of the English Working Class* (Harmondsworth, 1963; 1974 edition), pp. 734–68.

who was responsible for elaborating some of the most significant policies of this diplomatic body. Although Great Britain did not particularly favour the idea of sending European expeditions to help the Spanish recover their former possessions — an option frequently suggested by other European nations, especially Russia — neither did it make any special effort to approve the new Latin American states until the following decade.[16]

The ultra-conservative tendencies adopted by the Liverpool administration on both domestic and foreign fronts were subjected to persistent mockery and criticism by distinguished members of the British cultural elite. During his years of residence in London, Rivadavia was able to witness the increasing popularity, reflected in the very high sales of their works, of figures of the nation's literary scene such as romantic poets like Lord Byron (who, in accordance with a significant element of public opinion, passionately supported independence in both South America and Europe) and Percy Bysshe Shelley. It was these two poets in particular who were responsible for portraying Castlereagh as a symbol of what they considered the self-righteous and retrograde spirit prevalent in certain sectors of aristocratic society and the British political establishment. Shelley dedicated his poem 'The Mask of Anarchy' to this uncharismatic minister, two days after the tragedy at Peterloo, when he wrote:

> *I met Murder on the way*
> *He had a mask like Castlereagh*
> *Very smooth he looked, yet grim:*
> *Seven blood-hounds followed him.*

Byron, on the other hand, decided to leave England in 1816 and established himself on the continent, no longer able to tolerate what he viewed as rigid political, social and moral standards.

The Liverpool administration was also resisted by the Whigs in Parliament and by the Radicals, who in spite of their slight representation in the House of Commons were backed by a large number of

16   Kaufmann, *British Policy and the Independence of Latin America*, pp. 81–126; Gallo, *Great Britain and Argentina*, pp. 115–28.

people who did not yet enjoy the right to vote. However, these two political groups did not have sufficient popular backing to put the Tory majority at risk. In spite of the efforts of certain reformist Whigs and of the Radicals to promote parliamentary reform, which aimed at extending the right to vote in Britain, large sectors of English public opinion were still wary of these factions, not least for the enthusiasm that many of their members had shown for the principles of the French Revolution.[17] Rivadavia certainly disliked the approach of the ultra-Tory government of Lord Liverpool, which he described as '*profundamente antisocial*', although he also expressed his sympathies towards what he referred to as '*la nación inglesa*', presumably meaning public opinion, for their general support of the South American cause:

> It is by no means my intention to offend the English nation; she is, in the majority, in favour of our cause. On the contrary, it is necessary to establish a distinction between her and the government.[18]

Rivadavia also had words of praise for the Whig reformer Henry Brougham, for a speech Brougham delivered in the House of Commons in early 1817 where he attacked the Liverpool government for supporting the Spanish monarch Ferdinand VII and so disrupting Britain's commercial links with South America.[19]

During one of his visits to London, Rivadavia was introduced to Bentham and the principles of utilitarianism, which were to prove a powerful source of influence for his future political activity in the River Plate.[20] A number of South American agents on diplomatic missions

17 On this subject, see H.T. Dickinson, 'Popular Conservatism and Militant Loyalism 1789–1815,' published in *Britain and the French Revolution*, pp. 103-25.

18 'No estará por demás advertir que no se hiera ahí de ningún modo a la nación inglesa, ella está en lo principal por nuestra causa, al contrario es preciso hacer una formal distinción entre ella y su gobierno.' B. Rivadavia to J.M. de Pueyrredón, 22 March 1817. Published in Universidad de Buenos Aires, *Comisión de Bernardino Rivadavia*, vol. 1, pp. 196–214.

19 *Ibid.*

20 As will be discussed in the following chapter, a diverse group of historians seem to agree with this statement: Elie Halévy, who mentions the influence of Bentham's ideas on Rivadavia in his classic work *The Growth of Philosophic Radicalism* (London, 1928), p. 297; Piccirilli, *Rivadavia y su tiempo*, vol. 2,

to London at that time were also attracted to Bentham and other political and literary circles in the English capital.[21] After all, the English philosopher had been following the spread of republican ideals in emerging nations ever since the outbreak of the wars of North American independence. Moreover, he later wrote in favour of the newly established South American states, criticising Ferdinand VII's readiness to dismiss the principles of Spain's liberal constitution of 1812 and his attempts to recapture his empire's former South American colonies.[22]

On the other hand, works of Bentham such as *Traités de législation* published in 1802 and *Political Tactics* of 1817, translated into French and edited by the Genevan publisher Etienne Dumont, had by then already reached certain political and literary circles in South America. It is, then, quite likely that more than one publisher or politician in the River Plate was already familiar with these mentioned articles. The perception that Bentham already enjoyed a considerable reputation in Latin America is supported by remarks such as those made in

---

pp. 319–22; M. Williford, *Jeremy Bentham on Spanish America* (Baton Rouge, 1980), p. 20; J. Dinwiddy, 'Bentham and the Early Nineteenth Century,' in *Radicalism and Reform in Britain 1780–1850* (London, 1992), p. 304; K. Gallo, 'Jeremy Bentham y la feliz experiencia: Presencia del utilitarismo en Buenos Aires 1821–1824,' in *Prismas: Revista de historia intelectual*, vol. 6 (2002), pp. 79–96. A more sceptical view of this alleged influence can be found in J. Harris, 'Bernardino Rivadavia and Benthamite discipleship,' *Latin American Research Review*, vol. 33, no. 1 (1998), pp. 129–49.

21   Both J. Lynch (ed.), *Andrés Bello: The London Years* (London, 1982) and M.T. Berruezo León, *La lucha de Hispanoamérica por su independencia en Londres. 1800–1830* (Madrid, 1989), deal fully with this subject.

22   His most significant text in this respect, was 'Rid Yourselves of Ultramaria,' written around 1820, which was explicitly addressed to the Spanish monarchy, although it was not published until very recently in P. Schofield (ed.), *Colonies, Commerce and Constitutional Law: Rid Yourselves of Ultramaria and other writings for Spain and Spanish America* (London, 1995). Also worth mentioning on this specific subject are Williford, *Jeremy Bentham on Spanish America*; J. Harris, 'An English Utilitarian looks at Spanish-American Independence: Jeremy Bentham's *Rid Yourselves of Ultramaria*,' in *The Americas*, vol. 52, no. 3 (October 1996); Carlos Rodríguez Braun, *La cuestión colonial y la economía clásica: De Adam Smith y Jeremy Bentham a Karl Marx* (Madrid, 1989).

1824 by the famed English writer William Hazlitt who ironically said
that Bentham was better known in the Mexican and Chilean mines
than in Great Britain.[23]

One of Bentham's most prestigious acquaintances, James Mill,
had also published in 1809 a couple of articles in the *Edinburgh Review*
in favour of South American independence. These were written in
conjunction with Francisco de Miranda, the Venezuelan revolutionary who established contacts with the two philosophers before the
other emissaries sent from that continent.[24] Other Hispanic-
American agents besides Rivadavia and Miranda that Bentham met
at his Queen Square home in London were Simón Bolívar, José Del
Valle and José de Paula Santander, many of whom he later main-
tained correspondence with.[25] A particular 'incident' that took place
on the occasion of one of Rivadavia's visits to this celebrated house
drew the attention of John Bowring, Bentham's literary executor and
publisher of his first collected works, to such an extent that he tran-
scribed a description of this event in one of the volumes:

> When Rivadavia, the Buenos Ayres minister dined at his
> [Bentham's] table, he (a not uncommon trick of foreigners)
> spat on the carpet. Up rose Bentham, ran into his bed-
> room, brought out a certain utensil, and placed it at his vis-
> itor's feet, saying 'There sir, there — spit there.'[26]

23   Dinwiddy, 'Bentham and the Early Nineteenth Century,' p. 294.
24   These articles were entitled 'Emancipation of Spanish America', which
     appeared in January 1809, and 'Molina's account of Chile', which came out in
     July 1809; see J. Alberich, 'English Attitudes towards the Hispanic World in
     the Time of Bello as Reflected by the *Edinburgh and Quarterly Review*,' in Lynch
     (ed.), *Andrés Bello*, pp. 67–81. Mill had previously written a critical text, under
     the name William Burke, on the role of the British government during the ill-
     fated invasions of the River Plate, entitled 'Additional Reasons for our
     Immediately Emancipating Spanish America'. On this subject see J.
     Rodríguez, '*William Burke' and Francisco de Miranda: The Word and the Deed in
     Spanish America's Emancipation* (Landham, MD, 1994).
25   The correspondence between Bentham and Rivadavia, to be found in
     London at the archives of University College and the British Library, took
     place between the years 1818 and 1824.
26   J. Bowring, *The Works of Jeremy Bentham* (Edinburgh, 1843) vol. 10, p. 566.

Both Mill and Bentham were strongly opposed to the monarchic alternative for the South American nations. When, in 1819, Bentham became acquainted with Pueyrredón and Rivadavia's pursuit of European princes as possible candidates for an eventual River Plate monarchy, he did not hesitate to write an adamant letter to Rivadavia, then residing in France, alerting him to the evils that a monarchy would set off in that region:

> You wish for a king for Buenos Ayres and Chili: so at least,
> I understand from our friend Lawrence. If so, much good
> may it do you. But how much better would you be without
> one? The Spaniards have a reason, such as it is, for having
> a king. But you have not that reason — nor ever had.[27]

In spite of Rivadavia's association with Bentham, other South American diplomats residing in Europe were alarmed at his lack of interest in and excessive criticism of anything European.[28] Such was the case of the Chilean diplomatic envoy in London, Antonio José de Irisarri, who was particularly irritated by the Argentine's dismissive attitude:

> [Rivadavia] has four favourite phrases that he learnt from
> some book he read by chance, which are 'to be at the same
> level of the Enlightenment', 'the vagaries of politics', 'the
> philosophism of our times', 'the imbecility of the
> Europeans'. There is hardly a conversation, however trivial
> or short, where he does not repeat these phrases at least
> ten times, convinced that by doing so he will be considered
> an eminent orator. His idleness explains why he never vis-
> its anyone and never takes resolute steps in the matters of
> the business he was entrusted with. Up till now he has
> never seen the minister, nor has he attempted to see him.

27 J. Bentham to B. Rivadavia, 20 February 1819, British Library, Bentham
    Papers, Add. Mss. 33454. Reproduced and translated in R. Piccirilli, *Rivadavia
    y su tiempo*, vol. 2, pp. 438–40.
28 For the contacts made by South American agents with London political cir-
    cles during this period, see J. Dinwiddy, 'Liberal and Benthamite Circles in
    London 1810–1829,' in Lynch (ed.), *Andres Bello*, pp. 119–36; Berruezo León,
    La lucha de Hispanoamérica.

He has never been tempted to meet with the kind of people that could open up negotiations for him; and when I proposed to introduce him to the Duke of Sussex [George IV's younger brother] he told me he thought this gentleman would be of no use to him.[29]

This harsh account sounds somewhat excessive when one bears in mind the acquaintances Rivadavia managed to establish during his sojourn in England. However, it would appear that he did have certain contempt for aristocratic circles, as he probably had reason to believe that most of the British aristocracy was either prejudiced about or uninterested in the fate of the South American republics.

The Venezuelan Andrés Bello — who, alongside Bolivar and Miranda, had arrived in London in 1811 as part of his nation's first diplomatic mission since independence — was able to secure access to the prestigious political and literary circle of Holland House. Bello had contacted José María Blanco White, the Spanish priest exiled in England and the editor of *El Español* a journal sympathetic to the cause of the former Spanish American colonies. Through Blanco White he was introduced to the Whig circle commanded by Lord and Lady Holland.[30] However, Bello was to be one of the few South American visitors there, as Lord Holland, a leading figure of the

29 'Tiene (Rivadavia) cuatro frases favoritas, que aprendió en algún libro que por casualidad leyó y son: "estar al nivel de las luces del siglo", "el serpenteo de la política", "el filosofismo del tiempo" y la "imbecilidad de los europeos". No hay conversación por trivial que sea, ni por corta donde repite por lo menos diez veces estas palabras, creyendo que con esto se recomienda como un orador eminente. Su pereza no le hace visitar a nadie, ni dar un paso en los negocios que tiene a su cargo. Hasta ahora jamás ha visto al ministro, ni ha procurado verlo. Nunca ha tenido la tentación de hacer conocimiento con los personajes que puedan abrirle negociaciones; y cuándo yo propuse introducirlo al duque de Sussex, me contestó que no creía que pudiera servirle en algo este señor.'
Extract of a letter sent from A.J. de Irisarri to B. de O'Higgins, 14 March 1820. Published in Berruezo León, *La lucha de Hispanoamérica*, pp. 284–5.

30 On this subject see, for example, Dinwiddy, 'Liberal and Benthamite Circles in London, 1810–1829'; P. Grases, *Tiempo de Bello en Londres y otros ensayos* (Caracas, 1962); L. Mitchell, *Holland House* (London, 1980); M. Murphy, *Blanco White: Self-Banished Spaniard* (New Haven, 1989).

reforming Whig faction, had close ties with Spanish liberals such as Gaspar de Jovellanos among others. It is also important to note that the opinions of the members of Holland House towards the old Spanish colonies in America were extremely cautious, admitting at best a modest support of the emancipation of the new states. They were similarly distrustful of the republican experiments taking place in the region, and clearly considered a constitutional monarchy to be the more desirable political model, an alternative that was supported by Bello himself.[31] Blanco White shared Holland House's misgivings in relation to this subject, as was made clear in a letter he sent to Lord Holland in 1819 in which he expressed serious doubts about the South Americans' capacity to govern themselves.[32]

There is, however, no evidence of contact in London between Rivadavia and the Venezuelan or for that matter with Blanco White; it is highly probable that, given the disinclination of Holland House to admit South American agents, the River Plate emissary did not have an opportunity to visit that circle. In spite of his lack of contacts with representatives of the Whig faction, Rivadavia, as previously mentioned, had bestowed praise on Brougham, another frequent visitor to Holland House and regular contributor to the *Edinburgh Review*, the main organ for the diffusion of Whig ideals.[33] Brougham was strongly attracted to Bentham's projects in favour of judicial reform, but apart from his case and that of the Liberal-Tory Robert Peel, the utilitarian's ideas appealed mostly to moderate Radicals such as Francis Place. However, the latter faction, as we have noted, had practically no representation in the House of Commons.[34] Rivadavia's praise for Brougham appears to be a conse-

---

31   Mitchell, *Holland House*, pp. 217–39; Dinwiddy, 'Liberal and Benthamite Circles,' p. 131; I. Jaksic, 'Bridges to Hispania: Andrés Bello and José María Blanco White,' in C. Malamud (ed.), *La influencia española y británica en las ideas y en la política latinoamericana* (Documentos de Trabajo, Instituto Universitario Ortega y Gasset, 2000), p. 71.

32   Dinwiddy, 'Liberal and Benthamite Circles,' p. 130.

33   B. Rivadavia to J. M. De Pueyrredón, 22 March 1817, in *Comisión de Bernardino Rivadavia*, vol. 1, p. 204.

34   J. Dinwiddy, *Bentham* (Oxford, 1989), pp. 16–7.

quence not so much of his presumed admiration for the reformist's political ideals as of Brougham's public criticism of the Liverpool government for its support of Ferdinand VII, which he voiced in several sessions held in Parliament during 1816 and 1817, and for his evident approval of South American emancipation.[35]

In France Rivadavia became acquainted with reputed writers of republican inclinations such as Dominique de Pradt, Antoine Destutt de Tracy and also with the legendary Marquis of Lafayette, and he was able to observe the first six years of the Bourbon restoration in that country. His republican friends were not able to develop a prominent role in the opposition factions operating inside the reformed assembly. This space was to be mainly occupied by more moderate liberal groups such as the *Doctrinaires*.

In spite of the fact that Tracy pessimistically declared to Rivadavia that 'we poor Frenchmen are governed by the enemies of liberty and reason', one of the most interesting aspects of the political conjuncture was precisely the emergence of new factions in the re-established assembly.[36] The *Doctrinaires* managed to promote a most articulate opposition towards the Bourbons that would eventually prove vital in the downfall of that government in 1830. Certain intellectuals in this faction were instrumental in developing more moderate theories based on the principles of the 1789 revolution. This was manifest in the writings produced during these years by the leading mentors of this group, such as Pierre Royer-Collard and François Guizot, for whom it was essential to pay more attentive respect to customs and traditions, which they referred to as *les mœurs*, in order to understand how the political concepts they were invoking could more adequately be applied in post-revolutionary French society. This approach resembled certain elements of Edmund Burke's legacy in Britain, and particularly that of the Scottish Enlightenment tradition, picked up by the *Edinburgh Review*, which also held in common with the *Doctrinaires* a preference for constitutional monarchies over

35 J. Lynch, 'Great Britain and Spanish American Independence 1810–1830,' in *Andrés Bello*, pp. 15–16.

36 Destutt de Tracy to B. Rivadavia, 14 April 1822, quoted in Piccirilli, *Rivadavia y su tiempo*, vol. 2, p. 448.

republics, and of a gradual extension of the suffrage primarily destined to enlarge the vote amongst the so-called middling-ranks.[37]

On the other hand, French thinkers inclined towards more radical political tendencies, notably the *idéologues* like Tracy, Pierre Daunou and Pierre Cabanis, were not particularly impressed by the British liberal tradition. Tracy, for instance, went as far as to claim that this country was 'even less liberal than ours and is sustained more than anything else by its public spirit' in a letter sent to Rivadavia.[38] Like Bentham and James Mill, these men were also obsessed with the political developments taking place in the South American republics, which they viewed with expectation and a high degree of hope, tending to contrast their political situation with the conservative monarchical tendencies which had been re-established in their nation and most of Europe.

The pessimism that prevailed amongst many liberal politicians and thinkers in France with respect to the slim chances of a return of republican alternatives to government in Europe was expressed with much virulence to Rivadavia by Dominique de Pradt shortly after he had returned to Buenos Aires. Like Bentham, de Pradt thought it was totally inadmissible that the monarchic alternative had even been considered in the River Plate:

> If Spain did not have the means to resist you, it is because you were able to defeat her by the force of reason and arms. It is necessary to add to those examples you have given to the rest of the world those of moderation and unity. For a long time you have requested in London and Paris that your nation be recognised as independent. In those days your nation was weak, it had just been born; now that you can enjoy the plenitude of your rights do not recognise those who don't recognise you. Apply commer-

---

37   L. Siedentop, 'Two Liberal Traditions,' in A. Ryan (ed.), *The Idea of Freedom: Essays in Honour of Isaiah Berlin* (Oxford, 1979), pp. 153–74; F. Furet, *Revolutionary France 1770–1880* (Oxford, 1992), pp. 306–26; also P. Rosanvallon, *Le moment Guizot* (Paris, 1985).

38   Destutt de Tracy to B. Rivadavia, 14 April 1822, quoted in Piccirilli, *Rivadavia y su tiempo*, vol. 2, p. 448.

cial sanctions to those who delay their recognition. Do not fear Europe. It is so divided, weak and occupied in stupidities that you will be able to obtain what you want. Here no one thinks in America; only I bother to. Do not take your European princes, they will deceive you, like they have deceived us: in Europe anything notable becomes republican; all regal governments have been defeated and disinherited. Maintain yourself republicans, united, and strengthened by union. Leave us with our discords and pettiness.[39]

Considering how swiftly Rivadavia gave up all consideration of a monarchic alternative before leaving Europe, it does not seem too exaggerated to suggest that it may well have been the utilitarian lecturing he received from Bentham and Mill in England, and the republican rhetoric of de Pradt and the *idéologues*, that were partly responsible for steering the future Argentine president away from those schemes, redirecting him towards the essence of republicanism. It probably became clear to Rivadavia that the introduction of utilitarian guidelines in a republican government could support a more moderate political climate.

---

39   D. de Pradt to B. Rivadavia, 22 August 1822. Translation of letter written in French and quoted in Piccirilli, *Rivadavia y su tiempo*, vol. 2, pp. 462–3.

2

A Utilitarian Republic: The Government of Buenos Aires 1820–24

Rivadavia returned to Buenos Aires in 1820 to find his nation in a state of even more turmoil than when he left on his European mission six years earlier. At the beginning of that year, the United Provinces of the River Plate seemed destined to continue suffering the political strife that had been the norm during its first ten years of independent existence. In early February, the combined armies of Francisco Ramírez, the *Supremo* of Entre Ríos, and Estanislao López, Governor of Santa Fé, defeated the national army of General Rondeau at the battle of Cepeda. Both these provincial leaders had been former subalterns of Gervasio Artigas, the Uruguayan *caudillo*, who was one of the first pro-independence provincial leaders to resolutely defy the leadership of Buenos Aires.

As noted in the previous chapter, the tensions between Buenos Aires and the litoral provinces were directly related to the continual opposition of most of the interior provinces to the domineering centralism of the Buenos Aires governments, especially the control of the customs house by the capital. Immediately after the Battle of Cepeda, the triumphant *caudillos* imposed the Treaty of Pilar on the government of Buenos Aires. The treaty established a new confederate structure for the River Plate, which meant that local political autonomy would prevail in each of its provinces. Buenos Aires was now obliged to choose its own governor and elect a new provincial legislative assembly, a process of administrative reorganisation that almost immediately led to an extremely turbulent political experience in the province.

Competition for power arose between diverse *porteño* factions and gave way to a succession of governors being appointed and then dispatched, in what was to be labelled 'the anarchy of the year 1820'. In September a hero of the resistance during the British Invasions of 1806–07, General Martín Rodríguez, was made governor and managed to sustain himself in power after defeating his political enemies inside Buenos Aires. He wisely decided to sign the Treaty of Benegas, which marked the beginning of a long-lived truce between Buenos Aires and Santa Fé, which had become the most powerful province of the litoral area. Under this pact, both governments would assist the organisation of a constituent assembly composed of representatives from all the other provinces, with the express aim of re-establishing national unity.

One of Governor Rodríguez's main objectives was to confront the persistent Indian raids in the unpopulated rural areas towards the south of Buenos Aires. Another was the formation of a government of able politicians to whom he would entrust the task of redesigning a credible republican structure based on an organised and efficient state. This duty would eventually fall to Bernardino Rivadavia, who, in mid-1821, was appointed the Minister of Government of Buenos Aires.

Under the guidance of this political leader of the early post-independence phase, Buenos Aires would experience a rapid and sustained institutional transformation, mainly as a result of a series of economic, social and political reforms. The modernising and progressive measures enhanced the reputation of the government, especially amongst the rising British community of Buenos Aires. The main guidelines of the political programme put forward by Rivadavia would also, in certain respects, derive from a British influence: the utilitarian principles of Jeremy Bentham, who, as noted in the previous chapter, Rivadavia had met during his diplomatic experience in Europe.

Rivadavia and the 'Feliz Experiencia': the Utilitarian Dimension of the Buenos Aires Government Reforms, 1821–24

The influence exerted by Jeremy Bentham and his utilitarian ideas on Bernardino Rivadavia's political programme during the 1820s in Argentina has attracted the attention of several historians. The correspondence between the two men during the period 1818–24, and the reformist programme put forward by the latter as minister of government during the so called feliz experiencia in the government of Buenos Aires headed by Rodríguez between 1820 and 1824, is usually given as the most conclusive evidence for establishing Rivadavia's ideological affiliation to Bentham's ideals.

This alleged affiliation was the object of discussion by nineteenth-century Argentine writers and former presidents, such as Domingo Faustino Sarmiento and Bartolomé Mitre, among others. In a passage of a speech by the latter on the occasion of Rivadavia's birth centennial, 20 May 1880, he stressed the effects of Bentham's legacy:

> It was then [1820], also, when he [Rivadavia] took in the new ideas to reform the political and moral order from the original source of Jeremy Bentham's great inventiveness, [a man] who had been his teacher and friend — a great intellectual and bad writer like himself, freeing himself from the formalism and the restraints of routine, in order to walk assuredly and without any useless baggage along the wide road of modern progress and liberalism.[1]

Some years before, Sarmiento had somewhat ironically described, in his much celebrated literary work *Facundo*, the level of impact produced by the writings of the English philosopher on the incipient Argentine academic scene at the beginning of the 1820s, and the manner in which it was becoming a significant ingredient in the context of the hostile relations between Buenos Aires and the interior:

> 'By which author do you follow matters of legislation over there?', Doctor Jijena asked a young man from Buenos Aires. 'Bentham.' 'Who did you say? *Benthancito?*' he said, signalling with his fingers the size of the twelve volumes which Bentham's works had by then reached, 'Ha, ha, ha...by *Benthancito!* There is more doctrine in one of my books than in those hefty papers. What university and insignificant doctors you have!'[2]

---

1   'Fue entonces [1820s], también, cuando en la fuente original de ingenio profundo de Jeremías Bentham, su maestro y amigo — gran pensador y mal escritor como él [Rivadavia] — bebió las nuevas inspiraciones de la reforma en el orden político y moral, emancipándose del formalismo y de las trabas de la rutina, para marchar con paso atrevido y sin bagaje inútil por el ancho camino del progreso y del liberalismo moderno.' In B. Rivadavia, *Páginas de un estadista* (Buenos Aires, 1945), pp. 196–97.

2   '¿...Por qué autor estudian ustedes legislación allá?, preguntaba el doctor Jijena a un joven de Buenos Aires... Por Bentham. ¿Por quien dice usted?

In all probability, however, it was in Great Britain where evidence of the significant relationship between these two men was first unveiled, when John Bowring's tenth volume of Bentham's complete works, which included part of their correspondence, was published in 1843.[3] At the beginning of the twentieth century, Elie Halévy published in Paris his *La formation du radicalisme philosophique*, where he put emphasis on the widespread impact of Bentham's writings, and stressed the influence of his writings over Rivadavia. In the mid-nineteenth century, Ricardo Piccirilli dedicated a chapter of his biography on Rivadavia to the relationship, and at the beginning of the 1960s Sergio Bagú pointed out the significance of this association in a preliminary study to his anthology on the Rivadavian group's economic ideas.[4] In the 1980s, Miriam Williford published a book on the effects of Bentham's ideas in Latin America during the nineteenth century, emphasising his influence on Rivadavia, a point of view shared by John Lynch and David Bushnell in their work published during those years.[5] At the same time, however, John Dinwiddy argued that the scope of Bentham's influence in South America was limited, although he did point out that Rivadavia's case, and more specifically that of the reforms put forward by the government of Buenos Aires during 1821–24, was worthy of consideration and something of an exception.[6]

Some years ago, Jonathan Harris, a member of the Bentham Project, published an article in which he raised strong doubts as to the true extent of the utilitarian philosopher's influence over Rivadavia, despite the fact that the latter had been identified by

¿Por Benthancito?, señalando con el dedo el tamaño en dozavo en que anda la edición de Bentham…, ¡ja, ja, ja!… ¡por benthancito! En un escrito mío hay más doctrina que en esos mamotretos. ¡Que universidad y que doctorzuelos!' In D.F. Sarmiento, *Facundo* (Santiago de Chile, 1845; Buenos Aires, 1999 edition), p. 135.

3   Bowring, *The Works of Jeremy Bentham*, vol. 10, p. 500.

4   Halévy, *La formation du radicalisme philosophique*; Piccirilli, *Rivadavia y su tiempo*; S. Bagú, *El plan económico del grupo rivadaviano* (Buenos Aires, 1966).

5   Williford, *Jeremy Bentham on Spanish America*; J. Lynch, *The Spanish American Revolutions 1808–1826* (London, 1973; New York, 1986 edition), p. 72; D. Bushnell, *Reform and Reaction in the Platine Provinces, 1810–1852* (London, 1992).

6   Dinwiddy, 'Bentham and the Early Nineteenth Century'.

Bentham himself as one of his disciples. Arguing that the English philosopher was renowned for placing the label 'disciple' on a series of famous characters who approached him at one time or the other. Harris played down the importance that utilitarian ideas had had on Rivadavia and concluded that the way in which the Argentine suddenly distanced himself from his master, in the mid-1820s, reflected the weakness of this supposed ideological affiliation.[7] The former director of the Bentham Project, Fred Rosen, showed a similarly sceptical view in his work on the alleged influence of Bentham and Lord Byron in the Greek independence process.[8] In recent years, a series of studies published mainly by Argentine historians working on the diverse political, social and cultural trends in the Buenos Aires of the 1820s has once again taken note of the impact of some of Bentham's ideas and utilitarianism in general.[9]

The level of scepticism raised by Harris in relation to the somewhat exaggerated use of the term 'discipleship' to define Bentham and Rivadavia's relationship is certainly valid, but his article tends to disregard not only the references of political and ideological issues raised by these two men in some of their letters but also the presence of a diverse range of elements associated with the utilitarian doctrine that can be perceived in different spheres of the political, educational and cultural environment of Buenos Aires during most of the 1820s.

This chapter centres on some of the specific evidence that, in this author's view, underpins the argument that aspects of utilitarian thought can be clearly perceived in various reforms adopted by the Buenos Aires government between 1821 and 1824, and the fact that

---

7   Harris, 'Bernardino Rivadavia and Benthamite Discipleship'.

8   F. Rosen, *Bentham, Byron and Greece* (Oxford, 1992).

9   For example: J. Myers, 'La cultura literaria del período Rivadaviano: Saber ilustrado y discurso republicano,' in F. Aliata and M.L. Munilla Lacasa (eds.), *Carlo Zucchi y el neoclasicismo en el Río de la Plata* (Buenos Aires, 1998), pp. 31–48; F. Aliata, 'El teatro de la opinión: La Sala de Representantes de la época Rivadaviana,' unpublished doctoral thesis, Universidad de Buenos Aires; B. Davilo, 'De los derechos a la utilidad: el discurso político en el Río de la Plata durante la década revolucionaria,' in *Prismas*, vol. 7, pp. 73–99; K. Gallo, 'Un caso de utilitarismo rioplatense: La influencia del pensamiento de Bentham en Rivadavia,' in Malamud, *La influencia española y británica*, pp. 14–30; K. Gallo, 'Jeremy Bentham y la feliz experiencia,' pp. 79–96.

Bernardino Rivadavia was its key member can be no mere coincidence in this respect.

A Radical Twist: The Evolution of Bentham's Political Thought in the Early Nineteenth Century

According to Dinwiddy, Bentham's political radicalism grew stronger in 1809–10, during which period he revealed his commitment, through a series of articles, to parliamentary reform.[10] Thereafter, Bentham increasingly advocated republican systems of government consisting of democratically elected unicameral legislatures in preference to monarchic or aristocratic systems that, according to his opinion, represented a threat to the interests of the majority.[11] The English philosopher's inclination towards a more radical political stance is most useful to bear in mind when one considers the liberal dimension of the reforms mostly inspired by Rivadavia's Buenos Aires ministry.

Bentham's strong republican position would place him, within the English political spectrum, closer to the Radicals than to either Whigs or Tories, as both these factions, despite their ideological differences, emphatically defended a system of constitutional monarchy. It is worth noting, however, that the English philosopher's stance was more in tune with the milder political tendencies prevalent within the Radical factions. An advocate of this more moderate stance was Francis Place, the Radical leader who would later become one of the pioneers of the Chartist movement, and whose bookstore on Charing Cross Road was an important meeting place for English reformists when Rivadavia was residing in London.

By that time, Place had already distanced himself from the more extreme Radical publicists and activists such as Henry Hunt and William Cobbett. Place was increasingly wary of the political violence of the so-called 'London rabble', and he would gradually incline towards the idea of a closer alliance between artisans and reformists of the commercial middle sectors. He viewed Cobbett as too ignorant to envisage the need to promote this alliance between the lower and middle classes. These disagreements between the main rep-

10   Dinwiddy, *Bentham*, p. 12.
11   *Ibid.*, p. 81.

resentatives of the British radical tradition — thoroughly analysed by E.P. Thompson in his classic study of the origins of the working class in England — were to become more intense in the following years.[12]

Place became closer to Whig reformists such as Henry Brougham, who would eventually be persuaded by members of the main Radical committee in London, the Westminster Committee, to become a candidate for their faction in parliament.[13] As mentioned in the previous chapter, Brougham had become very attracted to Bentham's ideas, particularly those related to judicial reform, and despite Bentham's repeated criticisms of the Whigs Brougham frequently visited the philosopher's circle.[14]

Bentham's works, and particularly his style of writing, were frequently subjected to criticism from certain reviewers. In the *Public Register* of 1818 Cobbett, for instance, described Bentham's writing as 'puzzling, tedious and beyond mortal endurance', for its excessively dense and confusing style.[15] On the other hand, influential members of the Whig establishment such as Samuel Romilly reproached Bentham for his barely disguised republicanism, which emerged in his frequent attacks on the government, whilst James Mackintosh wrote a strong attack against Bentham's parliamentary reform project in the *Edinburgh Review* in 1818.[16]

It was in this article, anticipating the concerns that in the second half of the century would unsettle John Stuart Mill and Alexis de Tocqueville regarding the undesirable tendencies of democratic societies, that Mackintosh raised concern about the application of uni-

---

12   Thompson, *The Making of the English Working Class*; J. Stevenson, 'Popular Radicalism and Popular Protest 1789–1815,' in *Britain and the French Revolution*, pp. 80–81; for British radicalism of the beginning of the nineteenth century, see also M. Philp (ed.), *The French Revolution and British Popular Politics* (Cambridge, 1991).

13   Thompson, *The Making of the English Working Class*, pp. 670–1. See also R. Stewart, *Henry Brougham 1778–1868: His Public Career, 1778–1868* (London, 1985), pp. 89–91; B.M. Fontana, *Rethinking the Politics of Commercial Society: The Edinburgh Review 1802–1832* (Cambridge, 1985), pp. 135–7.

14   Dinwiddy, *Bentham*, p. 17.

15   Dinwiddy, 'Britain and the Early Nineteenth Century,' p. 295.

16   Dinwiddy, 'Liberal and Benthamite Circles,' pp. 124–5; Fontana, *Rethinking the Politics of Commercial Society*, p. 150.

versal suffrage, which he believed could degenerate into a tyranny of the majority.[17] Other contributors to the *Edinburgh Review* had no qualms about either branding James Mill as a 'Jacobin' or attacking Bentham for lacking common sense.[18]

The extent of the debate on suffrage in Britain in the first years of the nineteenth century is of particular interest in the context of the political reforms taking place in the early 1820s in Buenos Aires. A law of universal male suffrage was to be one of the first significant decrees introduced by the *Porteño* government, a measure that clearly showed Rivadavia's inclinations towards establishing democratic criteria in this new political phase.

A Reformist Agenda with Universal Suffrage as a Starting Point

The so-called Law of Universal Suffrage was one of the first reforms issued by the government of Buenos Aires, on 14 August 1821. It was approved, according to Marcela Ternavasio, in the expectation that its application could bring about discipline and order in *porteño* society.[19] According to Halperín Donghi, the expansion of suffrage provided a new dimension to the balance of power within the Buenos Aires elite, although power still depended on the political decisions of a small group.[20]

The electoral law established a minor division between the so-called 'active' voters — 'every free man, native of the land or settled in it, of 20 years of age or more, or before if he were already emancipated' — and the 'passive' ones — 'every citizen older than 25, who owns real estate or industrial property'.[21] There were also other divisions, such as the clause by which the Buenos Aires legislative assembly was assigned 12 representatives for the city and 11 for the

---

17 Dinwiddy, 'Liberal and Benthamite Circles,', p. 125.
18 Fontana, *Rethinking the Politics of Commercial Society*, pp. 92–3.
19 M. Ternavasio, 'Nuevo régimen representativo y expansión de la frontera política. Las elecciones en el estado de Buenos Aires: 1820–1840,' in A. Annino (ed.), *Historia de las elecciones en Iberoamérica, siglo XIX* (México, 1995), p. 68.
20 T. Halperín Donghi, *Revolución y guerra*, p. 382
21 *Ibid.*, p. 379.

province, creating, in José Carlos Chiaramonte's view, a kind of hier-archical distinction between urban and rural jurisdictions.[22]

The eminently liberal essence of this reform was supposedly a consequence of Rivadavia's influence, and notwithstanding its dis-tinctions, it clearly reflected the radical stance adopted by the govern-ment. This trend is particularly evident when compared to the restrictions still imposed by most European governments, particular-ly within the sphere of political rights and most specifically concern-ing suffrage during the same period, as Rivadavia's French mentors kept reminding him.[23] However, years later Esteban Echeverría, the renowned Argentine poet and initiator of the 'romantic generation', reflected critically on the electoral law proclaimed by Rivadavia's gov-ernment when he argued in 1846 that '*el vicio radical del sistema unitario, el que minó por el cimiento su edificio social, fue esa ley de elecciones: el sufragio universal*', which in his view was to blame for Juan Manuel de Rosas's seizure of power in Buenos Aires in 1829 and the political upheavals over the following quarter of a century, which would deeply affect the process of national unity until the mid-nineteenth century.[24]

Bentham believed that only a democratic system of government would prevent individuals from placing their personal interests over the rest of society. He also argued in his *Constitutional Code*, which he began writing in 1820, in favour of a republican and unicameral gov-ernment system with a democratically elected legislature, whilst the members of the judiciary and administrative authorities should be elected by legislators. He categorically rejected any idea of creating a

22   J.C. Chiaramonte, 'Acerca del origen del estado en el Río de la Plata,' in the Annual Register of the IEHS (Tandil, 1995), pp. 36–7.
23   I refer particularly to the more gradual and limited criteria held by factions such as the Whigs in Great Britain and the *Doctrinaires* in France during the same period. On this subject, see the classic work of Halévy, *The Growth of Philosophic Radicalism*. Also K. Gallo, 'Reformismo radical o liberal. La política Rivadaviana en una era de conservadurismo Europeo 1815–1830,' in *Investigaciones y ensayos*, no. 49, 1999.
24   'The radical vice of the unitary system, which destroyed the social structure's foundations, was that election law: the universal suffrage.' This excerpt comes from 'Ojeada retrospectiva sobre el movimiento intelectual en el Plata desde el año 1837,' in *Esteban Echeverría: Antología de prosa y verso* (Buenos Aires, 1981), p. 297.

second chamber because he thought that if it were not to be democratically elected it would not be able to veto the first chamber's decisions.[25] He also emphasised, as the radical British reformers had been doing for several years, that the basis of the electoral system should be sustained by four key principles: secret vote, male suffrage, equality amongst the electoral districts and annual elections.[26]

The electoral law of Buenos Aires failed to meet Bentham's requirements in relation to the equality between electoral districts and the secret vote. However, the introduction by the government of Buenos Aires of laws of universal male suffrage and direct voting for elections of the legislative assembly were clearly in accord with the English philosopher's ideas relating to this issue.[27]

There is no clear evidence, however, that the universal suffrage law fostered by Rivadavia was a direct consequence of Bentham's beliefs. In her exhaustive study on the evolution of suffrage in Buenos Aires during the first half of the nineteenth century, Ternavasio argues that the suffrage law put forward by Rodríguez's government had more to do with pragmatic motivations than with ideological inclinations that favoured the establishment of a democratic regime.[28] The absence of explicit reference to or invocation of Bentham in relation to this particular law would seem to support that assessment. Nevertheless, it does seem reasonable to suggest that it may well have still been a consequence of Rivadavia's association with Bentham. As has been pointed out, it was precisely during these years, and practically at the same time that these two men became acquainted with each other, that the English philosopher expressed his views in favour of an electoral system that was very rare in Europe at the time.

Abolishing the Archaic: Suppression of the *Cabildo* and Creation of a New Legislative Assembly

Determined to eradicate customs and traditions considered obsolete by certain members of the Buenos Aires elite, the *Cabildo* of that city

---

25   Dinwiddy, *Bentham*, p. 81.
26   Halévy, *The Growth of Philosophic Radicalism*, p. 259; Dinwiddy, *Bentham*, p. 82.
27   *Ibid.*
28   Ternavasio, 'Nuevo régimen representativo,' p. 92.

was finally abolished by the government, and in turn a provincial assembly was created. As Chiaramonte has suggested, the *Cabildo* seemed an anachronistic institution after the government decreed the creation of the new legislative assembly for the city, and when it was also planning a series of innovative judicial reforms.[29] Julián Segundo de Agüero, a key member of the Rivadavian group, argued at the time that abolishing the *Cabildo* corresponded to the 'urgency to do away with the "evil germs" that had to be destroyed'. This seems to imply, as Ternavasio has pointed out, that the government viewed the *Cabildo* as a useless institution, a remnant of the colonial period, which had been a source of the continuous factionalism that had provoked the political chaos during most of the previous decade.[30]

The architectural design of the new building of the Buenos Aires assembly matched, according to Fernando Aliata, the *Reglamento y policía de la Sala de Representantes*, which the Buenos Aires government had literally plagiarised from Bentham's *Political Tactics*, as Rivadavia himself would later confess in the last letter he wrote to the English philosopher in 1822.[31] Bentham had written that in order to carry out debates in an assembly effectively and without 'cheating', it was essential to introduce a series of architectural norms.[32] *Porteño* public opinion was made aware of Bentham's influence over the new building, when the local press specifically pointed out its architectonic similarities with the model of assemblies portrayed in his *Tactics*.[33]

29   J.C. Chiaramonte, 'Vieja y nueva representación: Buenos Aires, 1810–1820,' in *Historia de las elecciones*, p. 62.

30   M. Ternavasio, 'La supresión del cabildo de Buenos Aires: ¿Crónica de una muerte anunciada?', in the *Boletín del Instituto de Historia Argentina y Americana 'Dr. Emilio Ravignani'*, no. 21, 2000, pp. 69–70.

31   Aliata, 'El teatro de la opinión'; B. Rivadavia to J. Bentham, 26 August 1822, British Library, Add. Mss. 33545 in Piccirilli, *Rivadavia y su tiempo*, vol. 2, pp. 442–3.

32   For more on this subject, see Aliata, 'El teatro de la opinión,' pp. 11–12 and Dinwiddy, 'Bentham and the Early Nineteenth Century,' p. 304.

33   On this subject, Bentham declared that the hall had to have a 'circular shape with a short difference; a few steps such as an amphitheatre; the president's seat placed in such a way that he could see all the assembly...', in Aliata, 'El teatro de la opinión,' p. 12.

English residents in Buenos Aires were surprised by the harmonious functionality the new assembly seemed to be acquiring, such being the case of the first British consul in the River Plate, Woodbine Parish, who expressed much praise for the new building, whilst an anonymous English traveller who wrote *A Five Years' Residence in Buenos Aires 1820–1825* pointed to the fact that the speakers remained seated and would therefore 'not have the chance to shine over the rest'.[34]

Rivadavia enclosed a copy of the rules of the new assembly of Buenos Aires in the letter of 1822 to the English philosopher. When he received it, Bentham sent it to the Greek revolutionaries as a legislative model to follow:

> Legislators! Annexed is a present which I take the liberty to offer you. It is not merely what a work of my making would have been — a simple project and nothing more; it is a regulation, which already, during three years, has directed all the proceedings of a legislative assembly. This assembly is that of the Republic of Buenos Aires, in South America. The copy, for which I beg the honour of your acceptance, is probably the only one that now exists. The date, as you see, is wanting. It was sent to me by its author, Bernardino Rivadavia, in a letter dated 26 August 1822, and which, by some means, did not reach my hands until the 5th April 1824.

He added, with a certain degree of impudence, regarding the 'invaluable' document:

> Legislators! I send you these regulations [Rulings of the Assembly in Buenos Aires], and I have not even read them. This is the reason. There was no immediate motive for my doing so, and I have contented myself with causing an English translation to be made which I retain.

34 Woodbine Parish to George Canning, 12 May 1824, Public Records Office, Foreign Office Papers 6, hereafter P.R.O., F.O.; *Un inglés: Cinco años en Buenos Aires 1820–1825* (Buenos Aires, 1986), p. 23. Original title, *A Five Years' Residence in Buenos Aires During the Years 1820 to 1825: By an Englishman* (London, 1825).

Bentham's blind faith in Rivadavia's legislative project seems to further emphasise his already stated approval of many of the other government measures implemented by the Buenos Aires government.[35] After transcribing this letter in Bentham's *Complete Works*, Bowring concluded that, of all the South American representatives that Bentham had made contact with, Rivadavia was the one he respected the most.[36]

Those in Buenos Aires who sought to eradicate the political and cultural practices of the Spanish colonial past seemed to be in tune with the maxims of utilitarian thought. These norms were elaborated under a particular theoretical framework, which disregarded notions of natural rights that had gained a notable presence in the incipient *rioplatense* political arena, and they favoured the creation of laws of utility, more agreeable with the objective of promoting the greatest well-being for the greatest number in a society. In practical terms, according to Bentham, this goal could only be met if governments got rid of obsolete laws that undermined the social harmony and well-being of a community. In their place, it was essential to introduce more adequate laws which, as Mitre stated, would enable societies to 'liberate themselves from the formalism and obstacles of routine' and from a 'useless burden', which in turn would contribute to create habits and customs more in accord with a society attempting to promote greater equality and progress as well as the consolidation of a republican system.

Education, Religion and Public Opinion

Other reforms adopted by Rivadavia which may suggest the influence of utilitarianism were those applied in the spheres of religion and education. Also worth mentioning in this respect are the efforts made by certain publicists of the Buenos Aires government to promote ideas linked with the eighteenth-century Enlightenment and the expansion of cultural activities in the city. The Press Laws passed by the government in 1822 allowed for the creation of a greater

35   J. Bentham to the Greek Legislative Assembly, 21 September 1824, published in Bowring, *Works of Jeremy Bentham*, vol. 4, pp. 584–5.
36   *Ibid.*, p. 500.

number of newspapers and publications, which reflected an urge to broaden the scope of public opinion.[37]

The ecclesiastical reform was a major element in Rivadavia's agenda, its principal aim being the secularisation of the church. Seeking to uphold the pragmatic and rationalistic axioms of the Enlightenment tradition, the government justified this reform on the grounds that it was in the interest of both the state and society to restrict the church to its more specific functions. The restrictions eventually forced upon the Catholic Church included the suppression of most of the religious orders, the Act of Clergy Reform in November 1822, which among other things abolished ecclesiastical tithes, and the introduction of a law, two years later, which guaranteed religious freedom.

In his critical essay on Rivadavia's religious policies, Guillermo Gallardo held that he possessed a somewhat 'utilitarian view of religion', which he considered vital for establishing state order.[38] Bushnell acknowledged that the measures adopted by Rivadavia in this area represented his government's main 'package' of reforms, and that they were carried out with a greater degree of audacity than in other Latin American countries.[39] According to the same author, the ecclesiastical reforms applied in Buenos Aires and other Latin American countries during that period constituted an inconsistency in the liberal agenda of those leaders who believed in the need to restrict church freedom in order to secure greater levels of freedom among a greater number.[40]

According to Halévy, both Bentham and James Mill thought the tie that bound human beings to God was like that which bound the oppressed and oppressor, and they attempted to apply this unequal relationship to the political structure of their country.[41] In Dinwiddy's view, Bentham was essentially anti-religious, partly because he consid-

37   On the freedom of the press during the first decades after the revolution in the River Plate, see N. Goldman, 'Libertad de imprenta, opinión pública, y debate constitucional en el Río de la Plata,' in *Prismas*, vol. 4 (2000).

38   G. Gallardo, *La política religiosa de Rivadavia* (Buenos Aires, 1962), p. 228.

39   Bushnell, *Reform and Reaction*, p. 30.

40   *Ibid.*, p. 26.

41   Halévy, *The Growth of Philosophic Radicalism*, p. 294.

ered religion harmful to human happiness and partly because he was an empiricist who did not believe in the existence of God.[42]

As Roberto Di Stefano argues, the ecclesiastical reform fostered by the Rivadavians was essentially an 'experiment' which only took place in Buenos Aires, not in other Argentine regions except in a couple of provinces of the Cuyo area in the western Andean region — Mendoza and San Juan — owing to the closer ties established between the port city and Europe. Evidence of this was to be found in the notable increase in circulation of books written by European reformist philosophers that were debated in cafés and in political and literary circles of Buenos Aires at the time.[43]

The urge of the government of Buenos Aires to establish lay guidelines for *porteño* society was directly related to the need to introduce innovations in the sphere of education. According to Bentham, education was indispensable for the conversion of a nation to a utilitarian morality. He also thought the so-called Lancasterian system — under which more advanced students called monitors, supervised by masters, taught less advanced ones — was the ideal system to that end, mainly because it reduced costs and therefore made education more accessible for the lower classes.[44] In 1822, Rivadavia introduced this system, making it compulsory in public and private schools in Buenos Aires, provoking a reaction on the part of teachers who doubted the effectiveness of a system that placed so much responsibility on monitors and that represented an overload for them.[45]

---

42 Dinwiddy, 'Bentham and the Early Nineteenth Century,' pp. 298–9.

43 R. Di Stefano and L. Zanatta, *Historia de la iglesia argentina: Desde la Conquista hasta fines de siglo XX* (Buenos Aires, 2000), p. 209. For more recent approaches to this subject, see N. Calvo, '"Cuando se trata de la civilización del clero." Principios y motivaciones del debate sobre la reforma eclesiástica porteña de 1822,' in *Boletín del Instituto de Historia Argentina 'Dr. Emilio Ravignani,'* no. 24, 2003 and R. Di Stefano, *El púlpito y la plaza: Clero, sociedad y política de la monarquía católica a la república rosista* (Buenos Aires, 2004), pp. 193–214.

44 On this subject in particular, and on the development of education in Buenos Aires during the first half of the nineteenth century, see C. Newland, *Buenos Aires no es Pampa: La educación elemental porteña 1820–1860* (Buenos Aires, 1992), pp. 82–99.

45 *Ibid.*

Shortly afterwards, as if to fully endorse his trust in this type of system of education, Rivadavia sent two of his children to Hazelwood School, an experimental institution which Bentham strongly recommended, close to Birmingham in England, at the beginning of the 1820s.[46]

The University of Buenos Aires was created at the end of 1821, and the faculty members were chosen in February of the following year. The professor appointed for the civil law course was Pedro Somellera, who according to Juan María Gutiérrez, another member of the *Generación del 37*, taught 'with so much clarity and mastery Jeremy Bentham's ideas in matters of legislation, that the University of La Paz and the School of Cuzco, following Buenos Aires' example, adopted this course as a teaching text for its civil law courses'. A text including these lessons was published in Buenos Aires in 1824 as *Principios de derecho civil*, and Gutiérrez claims that its publication 'introduced the ideas of this famed reformer [Bentham] in the University of Buenos Aires'.[47] In 1822 Rivadavia informed Bentham that it was at his request that the course had been created.[48] Likewise, in his study on the English philosopher's influence during the nineteenth century in several continents, Dinwiddy acknowledges that Somellera's text was entirely based on Bentham's *Traité de législation*.[49]

However, the same degree of Benthamite influence would not be evident in the philosophy course dictated in the same university by the controversial clergyman Juan Manuel Fernández de Agüero. The strongest philosophical influence perceptible in the courses on this subject was that of de Tracy, who was frequently mentioned in Fernández de Agüero's text. Despite the already mentioned connection between the utilitarian and *Idéologie* schools of thought, there was no mention of Bentham and his doctrine in this text.[50]

The efforts of the government to impose public opinion on *porteño* society were in accordance with certain passages of Bentham's *Constitutional Code*, where he established the idea that public opinion

46 Williford, *Jeremy Bentham on Spanish America*, p. 103.
47 J.M. Gutiérrez, *Noticias históricas sobre el origen y desarrollo de la enseñanza pública superior en Buenos Aires* (Buenos Aires, 1998), pp. 417 and 546.
48 B. Rivadavia to J. Bentham, 26 August 1822, British Library, Add. Mss. 33545.
49 Dinwiddy, 'Bentham and the Early Nineteenth Century,' pp. 302–3.
50 Dinwiddy, *Bentham*, p. 83.

should be like an informal judicial body, referred to as 'public opinion tribunal', brought about through public meetings and the effective circulation of the press in social and political spheres. For Bentham it was essential to provide regulations allowing the promotion of legislative, judicial and administrative procedures established by the state.[51]

In his highly suggestive article on the role of the Rivadavian publicists during the *feliz experiencia*, Jorge Myers notes that the state of Buenos Aires consciously attempted to promote the press in order to generate customs considered appropriate for a republican society in a province where the development of institutions and norms of sociability were not yet fully developed.[52] The tenacious efforts of 'public writers', such as Ignacio Núñez and the poet Juan Cruz Varela, to shape a more conscious republican discourse by expanding the sphere of public opinion seemed to correspond with a utilitarian logic. The government also believed that in order to achieve consensus amongst citizens it was necessary to publicise its measures and decrees.

This trend, under Martín Rodríguez's government, developed into what Myers calls a 'Rivadavian literary culture', which, because it was mainly concerned with social and political issues, would not be strictly 'literary', even if some of Varela's poems, such as *Dido, oda a la libertad de la prensa, Corona de Mayo*, that mainly referred to the exaltation of patriotic epics and civic virtues, were indeed published. The publication of the works of this poet gradually enhanced the introduction of new European literary trends of exaltation of feelings and passions, which would pave the way for the emergence of romanticism in the River Plate in the following decade.[53]

In Bentham's view, poetry was an archaic genre, of little use for society and essentially incompatible with truth and precision.[54] Rivadavia was also critical of romantic authors such as Lord Byron, whom he defined as 'un inglés mal criado', and did not appear to

51   *Ibid.*
52   Myers, 'La cultura literaria del periodo Rivadaviano,' pp. 44–5.
53   *Ibid.*, p. 39. For the influence of Juan Cruz Varela's work during this period, see the classic biography of J.M. Gutiérrez, *Juan Cruz Varela: Su vida, su obra, su época* (Buenos Aires, 1918), pp. 173–240.
54   Dinwiddy, *Bentham*, p. 40.

have very much interest in literature as an artistic expression.[55] It would appear that the main reason for his support and promotion of Varela's poems was as a vehicle for the strengthening of certain political and social values.

As far as the reforms essayed by the government of Buenos Aires in 1821–24 in other areas considered vital by Bentham, such as justice and economy, it is more difficult to establish the precise influence of utilitarianism. The reform of the judicial system was Bentham's main concern because he considered it essential to separate the judiciary from the other two branches of the political system. According to Bushnell, Rivadavia had revealed that his objective was to realise the Benthamite ideal of simplifying the judicial structure.[56] However, in spite of certain reforms promoted by the Rodríguez government in the area of justice — creating the position of Justice of Peace both in the city and in the province of Buenos Aires and establishing a police department in those same jurisdictions — the complete separation of the judiciary was not achieved in this period.[57]

It is here worth mentioning Bagú's useful contribution on the economic tendencies of the so-called Rivadavian group. He refers explicitly to the influence of James Mill's *Elements of Political Economy*, which Rivadavia ordered to be translated in 1822, a year after its publication in Britain, and which introduced aspects of economic theory elaborated by David Ricardo compatible with some of the measures taken by Rodríguez's government, especially the reduction of custom tariffs. These measures were also in line with Bentham's commercial theory, but it is less easy to establish a similar association with other important economic measures such as the Law of Emphyteusis, which established the possibility of acquiring land formerly belonging to the Spanish Crown now that it was in possession of the state of Buenos Aires.

Shortly after hearing of Rivadavia's achievements in the Rodríguez government through the London newspaper *The Morning Chronicle* in 1824, Bentham wrote him a letter where he was unable to

---

55   Piccirilli, *Rivadavia y su tiempo*, vol. 1, p. 286.
56   Bushnell, *Reform and Reaction*, p. 21
57   Ternavasio, 'Nuevo régimen representativo,' p. 89.

disguise either his feelings of personal pride or some concern about his disciple's seeming indifference:

> Time after time accounts of your *res gestae* found their way into our newspapers: each time they exhibit the picture not merely of the greatest statesman late Spanish America has produced, but alas! The only one: and in this conception I have found myself confirmed by every opinion I have heard. At the same time, never has the pleasure produced by these cheering accounts been unalloyed, accompanied as it has been with the idea of my having been cast off by a disciple, if I may take the liberty of calling you so, of whom I have so much reason to be proud.[58]

By that time Rivadavia had left government and seemed more concerned about diplomatic settlements in London, and financing his mining projects in Argentina's northern territories. He no longer seemed interested in following Bentham's advice, although he did apparently visit him during his stay in London in 1824. However, two years earlier, in what would be his last letter to the English philosopher, Rivadavia summarised the wide variety of reforms he had contributed to as Secretary of the Buenos Aires government, indicating towards the end of that letter:

> You may be aware that I have devoted myself to reform all kinds of previous abuses that could be found in the handling of the Legislative Assembly, and the dignities that belong to it; to favour the establishment of a national bank on solid grounds; to reform, after awarding them fair indemnity, the civil and military employees who overburdened the state unnecessarily; to protect individual security through repressive laws; to put order and carry out public works admitted as useful; to protect Commerce, Science and the Arts; to bring about a Law approved by the Legislature to reduce Custom duties; to bring about in the same manner a much needed ecclesiastic reform which I

---

58   J. Bentham to B. Rivadavia, 5 April 1824. University College Library, Box XII.

have hopes of achieving: in short, to carry out all the worthy changes, which hopes of your honourable acceptance have given me the strength to promote and will give me the necessary [strength] to carry out. [59]

Although the identification of Latin American political figures who had some type of contact with Bentham as his 'disciples' may not be very helpful, this letter is certainly evidence of Rivadavia's attempt to promote a common ground between utilitarian philosophic principles and the reforms carried out by the government of the province of Buenos Aires in 1821–24.

59 B. Rivadavia to J. Bentham, 26 August 1822, British Library, Add. Mss. 33545.
'Así pues Vd. sabrá que me he dedicado a reformar los viejos abusos de toda especie que podían encontrarse en la administración de la Junta de Representantes y la dignidad que le corresponde; a favorecer el establecimiento de un banco nacional sobre sólidas bases; a reformar, después de haberles asegurado una indemnidad justa, a los Empleados Civiles y Militares que recargaban inútilmente al Estado; a proteger por leyes represivas la seguridad individual; a ordenar y hacer ejecutar trabajos públicos de una utilidad reconocida; a proteger el Comercio, las Ciencias y las Artes; a provocar una Ley sancionada por la Legislatura que reduce en mucho los derechos de la Aduana; a provocar igualmente una reforma eclesiástica muy necesaria y que tengo la esperanza de obtener: en una palabra de hacer todos los cambios ventajosos, que la esperanza de su honorable aceptación me ha dado la fuerza de promover y me suministrará la necesaria para ejecutarla.'

3

Reforming the Republic: The Cultural and Political Dimension of the Government of Buenos Aires, 1821–24

In his book on *porteño* society during the Rivadavian period, the anonymous Englishman defined the attitudes he found amongst the new generation as 'completely Voltairean', because of the lay inclinations and strong rationalist spirit that in his view were prevalent in certain sectors.[1] As we have seen, from the early nineteenth century the texts of various philosophers of the European Enlightenment arrived with increasing frequency in the port of Buenos Aires. Evidence of the circulation of this type of literature beyond the *criollo* elite emerged during the 1820s with the broad cultural initiatives introduced in Buenos Aires by Rodríguez.

The present chapter concentrates on the efforts made by the government, and particularly the so-called Rivadavian circle, to encourage diverse sectors of *porteño* society to act in accordance with the official slogan '*estar a la altura de las luces del siglo*'. Through the work of newspapers and associational groups the government sought to justify the ecclesiastical reform of 1822, transcribing in the press the debates in the *porteño* assembly regarding this issue. However, other forms of public representations were considered by the government to be equally important in this regard, and they actually encouraged popular events such as the *Fiestas Mayas* as well as the development of theatrical performance.[2]

1   Anonymous, *Un inglés: Cinco años en Buenos Aires (1820–1825)*, Colección Nueva Dimensión Argentina directed by Gregorio Weimberg, Editorial Taurus (Buenos Aires 2002), p. 184.
2   The term *Mayas* derives from *Mayo*, the month the first declaration of Argentine independence was decreed.
     For the government's efforts to foster sociability by extending associative groups and broadening the public sphere, see P. González Bernaldo, *Civilidad*

The 1822 Ecclesiastical Reform as a Generator of a Political and Cultural Debate

Much of the negative reaction towards this reform came from leading members of the clergy such as Mariano Medrano, Cayetano Rodríguez, Pedro Ignacio Castro Barros and Francisco de Paula Castañeda. They blamed those journalists belonging to Rivadavia's entourage for persistently promoting the anti-clerical precepts of the Enlightenment in order to generate a favourable attitude towards ecclesiastical reform. The highly critical stance adopted by these clergymen towards the reform was vigorously voiced in the heated debates in the Buenos Aires legislature during 1822, when Medrano, the Cathedral of Buenos Aires's Provisional Bishop, openly attacked the reformers, exclaiming 'Hypocrites! We already know who you are ... You destroy the places of piousness, you grab the church funds and you call yourself reformers?' In order to emphasise the tenor of his attacks, he also exclaimed: 'We already know you, fraudulent conspiracy ... You are disciples of Voltaire.'[3] Medrano employed the same critical language in reference to the negative role of what he called '*cierta prensa escrita*', which, endorsed by the government, had contributed to making public opinion favourable to the ecclesiastical reform:

> The press gave daily lessons of impiety, just as impunity authorised them. It was a treat to be libertine, and in the stre-

---

y política en los orígenes de la nación argentina: Las sociabilidades en Buenos Aires, 1829–1862 (Buenos Aires, 2001), pp. 36–90; Roberto Di Stefano, 'Orígenes del movimiento asociativo: De las cofradías al auge mutualista 1776–1860,' in E. Luna and E. Cecconi (eds.), *De las cofradías a las organizaciones de la sociedad civil: Historia de la iniciativa asociativa en Argentina 1776–1990* (Buenos Aires, 2002), pp. 55–66.

3   '¡Hipócritas! Ya os conocemos ... Destruís los establecimientos de piedad, os apoderáis de los fondos del culto y ¿os llamáis reformadores?'; 'Ya os conocemos, fraudulenta intriga ... Sois discípulos de Voltaire.' Both these quotes are cited in A. Tonda, *Rivadavia y Medrano: Sus actuaciones en la reforma eclesiástica* (Santa Fe, 1952), p. 86. See also K. Gallo, 'Mariano Medrano: El azaroso itinerario del primer obispo criollo porteño,' in N. Calvo, R. Di Stefano and K. Gallo (eds.) *Los curas de la revolución: Vidas de eclesiásticos en los orígenes de la nación* (Buenos Aires, 2002) pp. 121–41.

ets, the homes, and everywhere else, priests, but especially the devout, received insults, sarcasm, disrespect, scorn.[4]

Medrano's rage was directed towards specific publications that supported most of the Rivadavian reforms, such as *El Argos*, edited during its first year by Ignacio Núñez and in *El Centinela*, edited by Núñez and Juan Cruz Varela. The favourable attitude of these two newspapers towards the ecclesiastical reform could even be found in theatre reviews:

> In a farce called 'The Greedy Father', Culebras, in the Tramoyist lawyer's role, declared, 'there is little use for law in this day and age, especially if we are also subjected to a reform, such as the other privileged classes have undergone'. This unexpected outburst in the middle of a pretty ordinary and bland piece provoked an electric effect among the spectators, who laughed and applauded. Truly, this is no small proof that there is a desire for reform. It may be said that public recreation in our coliseum, which is composed of *magistrates*, PRIESTS, *legists, military men*, EMPLOYEES, *land owners and merchants*, and even those of the beautiful sex, offers the most exact representation of our people; and surely if it had been possible, in the play we refer to, to vote on the abolition of convents, there is no doubt that the majority would have risen [in ovation], supposing we include the suffrage of women, who are snubbed, as if they did not know the huge distance there is between virtue and the cloister.[5]

4   'Las prensas daban a diario lecciones de impiedad, al par que la impunidad las autorizaba. Se hacía un lujo de libertinaje y en las calles, en las casas, y en todas partes los sacerdotes, pero muy especialmente los religiosos, recibían insultos, sarcasmos, descortesía, desprecio.' Published in Tonda, *Rivadavia y Medrano*, p. 84.

5   'En una farsa titulada "El Padre avariento," dijo Culebras, en el papel de un abogado tramoyista; "poca utilidad ofrece la abogacía en el día y máxime si también viene por nosotros una reforma, como la que han sufrido las demás clases privilegiadas." Esta expresión inesperada en medio de una pieza bastante ordinaria e insulsa produjo un efecto eléctrico entre los espectadores, de quienes arrancó simultáneamente risa y aplauso. En verdad que esta no es muy corta prueba de que prevalece el gusto reformador. Se puede decir que

At the same time, the ebullient Franciscan Francisco de Paula Castañeda also attacked the government's reforms in newspapers that he himself published during those years. According to Juan María Gutiérrez, in his pamphlets Castañeda declared 'against "*philosophism*", against the fineness of the nineteenth century, against the books with "golden paste", against young people with "shiny boots", against Luther and Voltaire's supporters, against the enemies of the Church'.[6] These complaints against writers who exalted the benefits of ecclesiastical reform to *porteño* society reflected a deep concern amongst opponents who seemed to fear that the introduction of the reform would only promote values associated with the Enlightenment or Voltairean philosophy, as can be seen in another of Castañeda's diatribes:

> Let us learn the hard way, and let us confess that we lacked wise men before the revolution, and that through its lectures we have only managed to provide reverse wise men, or rather, wise monkeys from the foreigners, that is wise men who want us to proceed like the French, or the English, or the devil's way, just because trunks were taken and trunks were brought back from France, or from England. Let us wake up and confess to what Beresford said when he conquered this square, that is, *that the Enlightenment of South America was to be found in the clergy*; and I add that you shall also find in the clergy the prudence and

la recreación pública, en nuestro coliseo que es compuesto de *magistrados*, SACERDOTES, *legistas, militares*, EMPLEADOS, *hacendados y comerciantes*, y aún del bello sexo, ofrece la *representación* más exacta de todo el pueblo; y que seguramente si se hubiera podido, en el acto que se refiere, proceder a la *votación* sobre la abolición de los conventos, no cabe duda que la mayoría se hubiera puesto *de pie* al instante, suponiendo incluidos también a los sufragios de las mujeres, a quienes se ultraja, pretendiendo que ellas no saben la enorme distancia que hay entre la *virtud* y el *claustro.*' *El Centinela*, 27 October 1822.

6   'Contra el "filosofismo", contra la finura del siglo XIX, contra los libros de "pasta dorada", contra los jóvenes de "botas lustrosas", contra los secuaces de Lutero y Voltaire, contra los enemigos de la iglesia.' Gutiérrez, *Juan Cruz Varela*, p. 218.

the public concept that patriots never had, and that even if they did have it before the revolution, they surely lost it in the ten years of coming and going, doing and undoing, falling and rising, stealing and scheming.[7]

What particularly irritated Castañeda about the government's insistence in promoting Anglo-French ideals was that this was to the detriment of Spanish customs and values:

Let them make a bonfire in the middle of the square, and let Voltaire with his seventy volumes fall into it, for they have no use for us, then let Jean Jacques [Rousseau] together with Volney, Paine, the one who quotes and as many muddled books which have changed your judgement continue burning. Let Buenos Aires reform itself sacrificing official holidays, turning coffee shops into schools, and cards into notebooks and paper, that if we seriously set out to cure ourselves, we will be cured during the following decade. If we don't do it this way there will be no other alternative than that of the prodigal son: yes, gentlemen, Spain, which has been separated from us not by rebellion nor betrayal, but by circumstance, and the scandalous desertion of its kings, the Spain which we have never complained about as much as we do about ourselves; Spain and her bosom shall be the only asylum where we may be able to go when due to our own

---

7   'A fuerza de golpes desengañémonos, y confesemos que carecíamos de sabios antes de la revolución, y que en el discurso de ella solo hemos logrado proveernos de sabios al revés, o más bien diré, de sabios monos de los extranjeros, esto es de sabios que nos quieren hacer andar a la francesa, a la inglesa, y a la diabla, solo porque fueron baúles, y vinieron baúles de Francia, o de Inglaterra: desengañémonos, y confesemos lo que dijo Beresfor [sic]cuando conquistó esta plaza, a saber, *que la ilustración de Sud-América estaba en el clero*: y yo añado que en el clero está también la prudencia, y el concepto público que los patriotas jamás tuvieron, y que aún cuando lo hubiesen tenido antes de la revolución, seguramente lo hubieran perdido en los diez años de ir y venir, hacer y deshacer, caer y levantar, robar, e intrigar.' *Doña María Retazos: Francisco de Paula Castañeda*, Colección Nueva Dimensión Argentina, directed by Gregorio Weimberg, Editorial Taurus (Buenos Aires, 2001), pp. 219–20.

immorality the son chases the father with a dagger, the daughters the mother and when a guest is not sure of another guest because they are all thieves.[8]

The anti-reformist priest's obsession was with the 'Rivadavian literary culture' — the objective of which was to shape a new set of republican beliefs and establish the basis of a more stable political system.[9] There were, however, members of the church who took sides with the main arguments of the ecclesiastical reform. Among these were well-known Rivadavians such as Valentín Gómez, Julián Segundo Agüero — who had an active participation during the debates on the discussions of this reform — and Juan Manuel Fernández de Agüero. As we saw in chapter 2, the latter taught philosophy in the new University of Buenos Aires, a post from which he would be removed by the rector, the priest Antonio Saénz, who regarded Fernández de Agüero's teachings as compatible with 'sinful doctrines contrary to the Holy Religion of the state'.[10] However, shortly afterwards, the Buenos Aires government restored Fernández de Agüero to his position. The significance of this issue was expressed by *El Argos*:

> The rector has exceeded his authority, and in truth we were waiting to see if the government would agree this in a defin-

8   'Hágase una hoguera en medio de la plaza, y entre en ella Voltaire con sus setenta tomos, que para nada los necesitamos; después que siga chamuscándose Juan Santiago[Rousseau] en compañía de Volney de Payne[sic], del citador, y cuantos libros embrollones han transformado vuestro juicio. Refórmese Buenos Ayres sacrificando los días de fiesta, convirtiendo los *cafés* en *escuelas*, y las *barajas* en *cartillas* y *catones*, que si seriamente tratamos de nuestro remedio seguramente quedaremos remediados en todo el decurso de la década venidera. De no hacerlo así no queda más recurso que el del hijo pródigo; sí señores, la España, de quien nos han separado no la rebelión ni la perfidia, sino las circunstancias, y la deserción escandalosa de sus reyes; la España de quien jamás hemos estado tan quejosos como de nosotros mismos; la España y su regazo será el único asilo donde podremos acogernos cuando por nuestra inmoralidad el hijo persiga al padre con un puñal, las hijas a la madre y cuando un huésped no esté seguro de otro huésped a causa de ser todos ladrones.' *Desengañador Gauchi-Político*, 4 August 1820.

9   Myers, 'La cultura literaria del período rivadaviano,' pp. 31–48.

10   J.M. Fernández de Agüero, *Principios de ideología elemental, abstractiva y oratoria* (Buenos Aires, 1940), pp. 28–9; Gutiérrez, *Noticias históricas*, p. 103.

itive way in order for us to deal with the issue, and not with the doctrines, whose examination, approval or disapproval in the university as we know does not matter at all when it is a well known fact that every literate man in Buenos Aires has his shelves lined with themes of the same nature or worse. Regarding the doctrines we repeat, the only thing we have admired is, that in our present times people still insist in finding a way to proscribe them in order to keep the religion of Jesus Christ intact, without considering that such infernal intolerance has been its worst lashing. Additionally, in the midst of our satisfaction with the new position the government has adopted in this matter, we have hopes that it will continue to demonstrate that it [the government] acknowledges that it is there to rule, and not to obey anything other than the law.[11]

As can be seen, the ideals implicit in the ecclesiastical reform promulgated by the Rodríguez government were not only promoted in the

11 'El rector ha usado de una autoridad que no le compete, y á la verdad que nosotros lo que esperábamos era si el gobierno lo consentía definitivamente para ocuparnos de ello, y no de las doctrinas, cuyo examen, aprobación o desaprobación en la universidad sabemos que nada importa cuando es tan cierto que cada literato en Buenos Aires tiene en sus estantes erigida una cátedra de la misma o peor naturaleza. Respecto de las doctrinas repetimos, lo único que hemos admirado es, que aún se insista en este tiempo en adoptar el medio de proscribirlo para sostener intacta la religión de Jesu cristo, sin considerar que esa intolerancia infernal ha sido su mayor azote. Por lo demás en medio de la satisfacción con que advertimos la nueva posición que el gobierno ha ocupado en este negocio, nos lisonjea la esperanza de que continuará dando pruebas prácticas de que sabe que él está allí para mandar y no para obedecer, sino a la ley.' *El Argos*, 4 August 1824.
Regarding this matter, see also J. Myers, 'Las paradojas de la opinión. El discurso político rivadaviano y sus dos polos: el "gobierno de las luces" y "la opinión pública, reina del mundo",' in H. Sábato and A. Lettieri (eds.), *La vida política en la Argentina del siglo XIX: Armas, votos y voces* (Buenos Aires, 2003), pp. 83–6; on the creation of the University of Buenos Aires, T. Halperín Donghi, *Historia de la Universidad de Buenos Aires* (Buenos Aires, 1962, second edition 2002), pp. 9–40; on the student atmosphere at the time, González Bernaldo, *Civilidad y política en los orígenes de la nación argentina*, pp. 88–90.

press but also by Rivadavians in the university, generating a strong debate within *porteño* society. The fierce irruption of these antagonisms was one of the objectives sought by Rivadavia's circle in order to diversify opinion in the public arena. Consequently, and with the express intention of swinging opinion in favour of its reforms, the government supplemented the efforts of its publicists and supporters by organising public ceremonies to exalt their main reforms through visual and symbolic manifestations, hence the significant dimension acquired by civic festivities and theatrical representations during this period.

Regenerating the Republican Society through Imagery

Since the partial proclamation of River Plate independence in May 1810, the civic festivities — celebrations which were also a main feature of public life during colonial times — would become one of the main attractions in the River Plate provinces. Recent studies have shown that, in the political context of the recently transformed territory, these festivities acquired a new significance because of the need of the first *criollo* governments to obtain greater popular acceptance of independence.[12]

When Martín Rodríguez's government was established in 1820, major modifications were made to the organisational guidelines of the festivities. Unlike the previous decade, when ceremonies were organised and supervised informally by citizens' commissions dependent upon the *Cabildo*, from 1821 onwards they would be planned by two agencies created by the government: the Engineering Architects and Provincial Police.[13] In that year, a French architect by the name of Próspero Catelin, who had arrived in Buenos Aires four years earlier, was appointed director of the Department of Engineering Architects. This new civil servant would be in charge of

12 See J.C. Garavaglia, 'A la nación por la fiesta: Las *Fiestas Mayas* en el origen de la nación en el Plata,' in *Boletín del Instituto de Historia Argentina 'Dr. Emilio Ravignani*,' no. 22 (2000), pp. 73–100; and M.L. Munilla Lacasa, 'Celebrar la "feliz experiencia",' in her doctoral thesis 'Celebrar y gobernar: Un estudio de las fiestas populares en Buenos Aires 1810–1835' (Universidad de Buenos Aires, not yet published).

13 Munilla Lacasa, 'Celebrar la "feliz experiencia",' p. 6.

organising the *Fiestas Mayas* of 1822 to commemorate the independence declared by the *rioplatense* Creoles on 25 May 1810.

According to several accounts of the time, the patriotic festivities of 1822 were notable for the incredible array of lighting and fireworks employed. The enthusiasm with which John Murray Forbes, the North American diplomatic agent commissioned in Buenos Aires, described these festivities to the Secretary of State John Quincy Adams would seem to corroborate that account:

> As we agreed, the government's subordinate came to my home at 8, in his carriage, to conduct me to the official residence, from where I accompanied him to the *cabildo* balconies, the most important public building, facing the great square. I was given a central seat in this balcony, from where I was able to see the most splendid event I have ever seen. Shining lights, the square and the adjacent houses filled with dames and gentlemen, the former of great beauty and elegance, and the fireworks as good as any I have seen in Europe.[14]

Another highlight of these festivities was the temporary architectural structures with monumental columns, which corresponded to a neoclassical aesthetic, especially designed and built on the *Plaza de la Victoria* by Catelin himself. As María Lía Munilla suggests, it is probable that Catelin had been inspired by his recollections of the civic festivities staged in Paris in the years of the French Revolution during the 1790s, of which thorough descriptions can be found in the works of Lynn Hunt and Mona Ozouf. As in the Parisian festivities, the Mayan celebrations were marked by invocations to certain deities of Ancient Rome, including the exaltation of Jupiter's image. It seems clear that these particular forms of artistic representation signified a conscious effort to articulate symbols of republican values and the principles of the European Enlightenment.[15]

14   John M. Forbes to John Q. Adams, 10 July 1822, in J.M. Forbes, *Once años en Buenos Aires* (Buenos Aires, 1956), p. 182.

15   Munilla Lacasa, 'Celebrar la "feliz experiencia",' pp. 25–6; L. Hunt, *Politics, Culture and Class in the French Revolution* (California, 1984); M. Ozouf, *La fête revolutionnaire 1789–1799* (Paris, 1976).

It is very likely that the political and ideological message the government sought to transmit via these representations may not have been entirely grasped by a large part of the crowd that attended these festivities. Nevertheless, it is plain that the government sought to promote the ideals of the Enlightenment to *porteño* society by way of allusive artistic imagery.[16] The popularity of these festivities contrasted, according to the chronicles of a Scottish commercial agent, with the apparently diminishing enthusiasm and increasing indifference that many *porteños* displayed towards religious ceremonies, particularly those which took place in the streets, such as the Corpus Christi procession. According to the Scot, this attitude corresponded to the citizens' 'good practical sense' and 'inclinations towards commerce'.[17] Similar accounts were expressed by the anonymous Englishman, who stated that any Spaniard who returned to Buenos Aires after being absent from the city for some time would be surprised by the way the 'rigid Church festivities had been replaced by innocent distractions'.[18] Likewise, this anonymous author was perplexed by the absence of official receptions or ceremonies, and by the great degree of indifference and contempt shown by large sectors of the population on the occasion of the visit to Buenos Aires in the first days of 1824 of a mission sent by the Vatican, headed by Cardinal Muzi and which also included Giovanni María Mastai Ferreti, the future Pius IX. According to the Englishman, such indifference towards a visit from a Vatican representative would have been unimaginable only a short time before.[19] However, the highly critical tone and irritation manifested in the chronicle of *El Argos* is proof that there probably was not such indifference after all:

> The whole town seems to be talking about this affair in the last fifteen days, and it has arrived at the conclusion that it is uncertain that the so-called Mr. Juan Musi has the high rank which is accorded to him, because they assure that, even if he has donned in this same city an archbishop's garments, he has

16   Munilla Lacasa, 'Celebrar la "feliz experiencia",' pp. 30–4.
17   J.P. and W.P. Robertson, *Cartas de Sudamérica*, (Buenos Aires, 2000), p. 395.
18   *An Englishman*, p. 94.
19   *Ibid.*, p. 184.

not presented any title, nor even the [permission] which should authorise him to preside over Mass. If this is true, as is generally affirmed, we don't know the reason why Mr. Musi has been allowed to administer the sacrament of confirmation in private homes, been admitted as a visitor, walking around the streets, using the privilege of blessing, which may only be used by those prelates who are legally authorised.[20]

The sustained efforts made by the government and the Rivadavian group to promote public festivities instead of the traditional religious festivities partly represented a programme of regeneration to mould republican values and customs in a society severely affected by the political vicissitudes of the previous decade.

These goals were reminiscent of the cultural reformulation of the Jacobins in France after the Republic had been proclaimed in 1792, allowing for the obvious differences between that political faction and the Rivadavian group in Argentina. It is worth noting that Castañeda assiduously made reference to the 'Jacobin ministry in Buenos Aires' in his passionate attacks on the Rodríguez government.[21]

Theatre as an 'Enlightened' Representation of the Rivadavian Reformist Programme

As has been noted, Ignacio Núñez was the writer of the Rivadavian group who was most strongly identified with the government's

20   'Toda la ciudad parece haberse ocupado de este incidente, en los ultimas quin-
ce días, y arribado por fin a dudarse absolutamente si el tal señor Juan Musi
[sic] es o no, revestido de aquel elevado carácter, que se le atribuye, porque se
asegura que, a pesar de haberse vestido en esta misma ciudad del ropaje arzo-
bispal, no ha presentado titulo alguno ni aún siquiera el que debiera autorizar-
le para decir misa. Si esto es cierto, como generalmente se afirma, no se atina
el motivo, por que se ha permitido que el señor *Musi* haya administrado el
sacramento de la confirmación, en casas particulares, admitido en visita, pase-
ándose por las calles, ejerciendo la prerrogativa de la bendición, de que sólo
pueden usar los prelados legalmente constituidos.' *El Argos*, 17 January 1824.
On this issue see also V. Ayrolo, 'Una nueva lectura de los informes de la
misión Muzi: La Santa Sede y la Iglesia de las Provincias Unidas,' in *Boletín del
Instituto de Historia Argentina 'Dr. Emilio Ravignani'*, no. 14 (1996), pp. 31–60.
21   *Doña María Retazos*, 1 August 1823, in *Doña María Retazos*, p. 309.

reformist agenda. In accordance with the government's objective of eradicating anachronistic practices, Núñez argued strongly in favour of the abolition of bullfighting. The prohibition of this sport, eventually achieved in 1822, was a consequence of it being considered an excessively bloody spectacle that did not align with the main guidelines of the 'Partido del orden' for the sphere of popular culture. In exchange for this sport, which he scornfully described as 'only practised in Spain', Núñez considered the theatre as a much more appropriate recreational activity for families.[22] This somewhat patronising approach towards anything Spanish was evident in one of the newspapers he himself edited, in the form of a series of sarcastic remarks about theatrical tradition in Spain: 'And the *tonadilla?* and the *saynete?* Oh! Why ask such questions! That one … too salty for the populace's taste … Both dull and indecent.'[23] The same newspaper frequently made reference to the advanced aesthetic judgement of the *porteño* theatre audience, for example when, on a certain occasion, it expressed strong disapproval of archaic forms of theatrical representation:

> After the presentation of the first of the two musical pieces, the *patio* [audience] finally expressed in very clear terms its well-deserved disgust for the reputation of one of those old-fashioned *tonadillas*, the lyrics, music and performance of which clash equally, and they are capable of making the foreigners think that we are tone-deaf and have no common sense nor shame. When they burnt the instruments of torture in the public square, they, should have burnt them with these *tonadillas* so that they would no longer torment us.[24]

22　J. Myers, 'Una revolución en las costumbres: Las nuevas formas de sociabilidad de la elite porteña, 1800–1860,' in F. Devoto and M. Madero (eds.), *Historia de la vida privada en la Argentina* (Buenos Aires, 1999), p. 125.

23　'¿Y la tonadilla y el saynete? ¡Ah! ¡para que esta pregunta! Aquella…salada el paladar del populacho … Á la vez insulso e indecente.' *El Argos*, 9 June 1821.

24　'Después de la representación de la primera de las dos piezas expresó, por fin, el patio, en términos nada equívocos, su bien merecido disgusto a la reputación de una de esas *tonadillas* a lo antiguo, cuya letra, música, y ejecución chocan igualmente, y son capaces de hacer creer á los forasteros que no tenemos oídos, sentido común, ni vergüenza. Cuando se quemaron en la plaza pública los instrumentos de la tortura, con estas tonadillas se hubiera debido encender la pieza, para que no volviesen a *atormentarnos* más.' *El Argos*, 11 September 1822.

It was precisely to the theatrical milieu of Buenos Aires that the anonymous Englishman made reference when he identified the lay tendencies of certain sectors of *porteño* society, pointing out the occasions on which cheers and applause would inevitably fall upon an actor playing the part of Voltaire.[25] In 1821, José de San Martín expressed words in favour of the theatre, which he considered as 'a moral and political establishment of greater utility' necessary for asserting the ideals of independence.[26]

Even though bullfighting was popular in Buenos Aires, its eradication did not seem to provoke major complaint. It is practically impossible to determine to which other shows or modes of entertainment the old bullring crowd were diverted, but a number of accounts reflect decent attendance at the theatre during those years.[27] There is also evidence which suggests that, in spite of the existence of preferential seats and boxes, theatre attendees came from diverse social sectors.[28]

It was clear in the years immediately after the 1810 Revolution that there was a strong inclination, especially amongst some of the more radicalised politicians, towards theatre. Such were the cases of Bernardo de Monteagudo, the Chilean clergyman Camilo Henríquez, author of several plays which were represented in Buenos Aires during those years, and Manuel Moreno, younger brother of Mariano.[29] Even though, as Beatriz Seibel reminds us, the theatrical profession

25   *An Englishman*, p. 184.
26   B. Seibel, *Historia del teatro argentino: Desde los rituales hasta 1930* (Buenos Aires, 2002), p. 69.
27   J.P. and W.P. Robertson, *Cartas de Sudamérica*, p. 392; *An Englishman*, p. 92; Seibel, *Historia del teatro argentino*, p. 81. For a more detailed survey on the theatre scene during this period see O. Pellettieri (ed.), *Historia del teatro argentino en Buenos Aires*, 7 vols. (Buenos Aires, 2005), vol. 1, pp. 141–270; E. Molina, 'Pedagogía cívica y disciplinamiento social: representaciones sobre el teatro entre 1810 y 1825,' *Prismas*, vol. 8 (2004), pp. 33–58; K. Gallo, 'Un escenario para la "feliz experiencia": Teatro, política y vida pública en Buenos Aires 1820–1827,' in G. Batticuore, K. Gallo and J. Myers (eds.), *Resonancias románticas: Ensayos sobre historia de la cultura argentina (1820–1890)* (Buenos Aires, 2005), pp. 121–34.
28   Myers, 'Una revolución en las costumbres,' p. 123; Seibel, *Historia del teatro argentino*, pp. 79–81.
29   Molina, 'Pedagogía cívica y disciplinamiento social,' pp. 33–58.

still had an 'infamous reputation' in the River Plate, some individuals who were very close to Rivadavia's circle, such as Valentín Gómez, Santiago Wilde and Esteban de Luca, had sponsored in 1817 the establishment in Buenos Aires of *La Sociedad del Buen Gusto y el Teatro*.[30] The members of this organisation attempted to foster the improvement of an artistic endeavour, which they referred to as 'school of customs and best teacher of the Enlightenment', and favoured the French and Italian dramaturgy — with plays which exalted freedom and hatred of tyranny, such as Voltaire's *Caesar's Death* or Alfieri's *Free Rome* — in preference to plays from the Spanish Golden Age.[31]

As Myers argues, most members of that society tended to perceive the theatre more as a didactic instrument, intended for a mostly illiterate population, than as entertainment.[32] The evidence of increasing interest towards more advanced modes of theatrical representation in the city of Buenos Aires alarmed Castañeda, who considered that they further emphasised the anti-Spanish tendencies of the government of Buenos Aires, as he claimed in typically inflammatory fashion:

> Theatre in Buenos Aires is an imitation of the country's progress, and in effect we have noticed that it is progressing and developing in direct proportion to our political system; what I mean to say is that it has been corrupting itself while we have been growing further away from the true Castilian virtue which was our national virtue, and was our true, noteworthy, and celebrated character; our revolution was, no doubt, the most sensible, the most honoured, the most noble of all revolutions there ever have been in this world as it did not limit itself to reforming our very corrupt administration and to governing ourselves in case Fernando did not return to the throne, or did not accede to our fair demands.[33]

---

30 Seibel, *Historia del teatro argentino*, p. 69.

31 *Ibid.*, pp. 60–1.

32 Myers, 'Una revolución en las costumbres,' pp. 123–4.

33 'El teatro de Buenos Aires es émulo de la patria en sus progresos, y en efecto hemos notado que progresa, y avanza en razón directa de nuestro sistema político; quiero decir que se ha ido corrompiendo a proporción que hemos ido

It was clear that the Rivadavian group was seeking to improve the quality of the theatre. From the 1822 decrees under which, together with the creation of the Literary and Musical Societies, Rivadavia ordered the establishment of the Reciting and Dramatic School 'to improve the profession of theatre actors not only to the perfection determined by good taste, but to the decency which contributes to hold up the principles which should exist in the whole country'.[34] The minister was also responsible for promoting Juan Cruz Varela's literary and theatrical works, of which *Dido* probably was one of the most acclaimed. This play was read in public for the first time by the author himself at Rivadavia's house, in front of members of the government, foreign attachés and representatives of the cultural elite; later it was staged in the theatre in front of larger audiences. Some newspapers, such as *El Argos*, felt a need to praise Varela's play not only because it was evidence of the efforts being made to promote a so-called 'national theatre', but also because it was a tragedy:

> Dido's tragedy, which has recently been offered to the public by Mr. D. Juan C. Varela, is a great honour to Buenos Aires, and even to all of America. A good production in this genre has always been considered a great sign of genius. As tragedy is the representation of a heroic deed, designed to inspire terror and compassion, and because in the cultured times in which we live, nothing appeals without that delicacy in taste, which is an effect of a sensitive and voluptuous emotion, it is necessary that the author use all of passions' expressiveness and dress the tragic Muse with all the grace of simple

---

alejando de la verdadera virtud castellana que era nuestra virtud nacional, y formaba nuestro verdadero apreciable, y celebrado carácter; nuestra revolución fue sin duda la más sensata, la más honrada, la más noble de cuantas revoluciones ha habido en este mundo pues no se redujo más que a reformar nuestra administración corrompidísima y a gobernarnos por nosotros mismos en el caso que o Fernando no volviese al trono, o no quisiese acceder a nuestras justas reclamaciones.' *El Desengañador Gauchi-Político*, 10 August 1820.

34   'Para elevar la profesión de los actores dramáticos no sólo a la perfección que regla el buen gusto sino a la decencia que contribuye a hacer efectivo el principio que debe dominar en todo el país.' Seibel, *Historia del teatro argentino*, p.72.

nature. Tears have also their pleasure and beauty; sometimes they are sweeter and more beautiful than laughter.[35]

Some of the travellers' chronicles of that period praised the merits
of actors and actresses of the *porteño* stage and, as has already been
mentioned, it was now usual to find theatre reviews, especially in *El
Argos*, a genre which had only recently sprung up in European nations,
where this artistic activity was far more ancient. Explicit reference was
made to the differences between lyrical and dramatic actors, some of
whom enjoyed great popularity in the city, such being the cases of
Trinidad Guevara, Angelina Tanni, the Spaniard Mariano Pablo
Rosquellas, also a theatrical entrepreneur, and the comedian Culebras.
It was the first of these performers, 'la Trinidad' as she was commonly
known, a protégée of the members of the *Sociedad del Buen Gusto y el
Teatro* and of the writers of the main newspapers, who would be at the
centre of a much-publicised quarrel with Father Castañeda in 1821. As
has been seen, at that time Castañeda was devoted to writing inflammatory articles against the Rivadavian reforms. He used these columns to
condemn the escalating circulation and influence of authors such as
Rousseau and the imported trends from Europe prevalent in certain
porteño intellectual and political circles, and in his highly acclaimed *Tres
comedias de Doña María Retazos* he displayed his profound disdain for theatrical representation.

In his clash with 'La Trinidad', Castañeda had denounced her for
wearing a necklace that held a medallion with the face of a man with
whom he claimed the actress was having an extramarital affair. The
lover was suspected of being Manuel Bonifacio Gallardo, a lawyer
and politician who was during most of the 1820s a deputy in the

---

35 'Hace mucho honor a Buenos Aires, y aún a toda la América la tragedia Dido,
    que acaba de dar al público el Sr. D. Juan C. Varela. Siempre se ha mirado una
    buena producción de este género por uno de los grandes esfuerzos del genio.
    Como la tragedia es la representación de una acción heroica, destinada a
    infundir el terror y la compasión; como en los tiempos cultos en los que vivi-
    mos, nada agrada sin esa delicadeza de gusto, que es el efecto de un sentimien-
    to sensible y voluptuoso, es preciso que para su autor toda la elocuencia de
    las pasiones, y vista á la Musa trágica con todas las gracias de la sencilla natu-
    raleza. Tiene también el llanto su placer y su gala, á veces más dulce y bello
    que la risa.' *El Argos*, 6 September 1823.

House of Representatives, very close to the Rivadavian intellectual circles, a fact that would partly explain the priest's irritation. In view of this affair, Castañeda had no qualms in calling 'La Trinidad' *'una cloaca de vicios e inmundicias'*, a sewer of vice and filth, which provoked her to accuse him of spreading an 'inflammatory libel' which at any rate would force her to stop acting for some time.[36] It is rather suggestive that Trinidad Guevara referred to Castañeda's accusations as a 'black revenge' by which she had been subjugated before 'a cultured people' from whom she expected nothing but understanding.[37]

The actress's expectations seem to have been fully met when she was highly praised on her return to the stage after her short exile. Unsurprisingly, *El Argos* cheered this event:

> La *Trinidad* (whose emergence on stage the public celebrated in spite of her defenders' indiscreet verses and prose) held the piece in true *dramatic* style. In order to persuade the public that she has merits on stage, this lady did not need the praises of the wretched poet who insists on convincing us that *dullness has ceased* when his own verses prove the opposite.[38]

A similar satisfaction with the successful comeback of the actress to the stage was expressed by the anonymous Englishman, who also described the details of the above-mentioned incident, praising the *porteños* for being wise enough to judge public and private affairs as separate things.[39]

---

36   Seibel, *Historia del teatro argentino*, p. 68; A. Taullard, *Historia de nuestros viejos teatros* (Buenos Aires, 1832), pp. 91–2; L. Ordaz, 'Nacimiento del teatro,' in S. Zanetti, *Historia de la literatura argentina: Desde la colonia hasta el romanticismo* (Buenos Aires, 1980–86), p. 330; R.H. Castagnino, *El teatro en Buenos Aires durante la época de Rosas* (Buenos Aires, 1944), p. 77–84.

37   Seibel, *Historia del teatro argentino*, p. 68

38   'La *Trinidad* (cuya salida celebró el público á pesar de la indiscreción de sus defensores en sus versos y en su prosa) sostuvo la pieza en el verdadero estilo *dramático*. Esta señora no necesitaba para persuadir al público que tiene méritos en las tablas, de los elogios de un miserable versista que se empeña en convencernos que ha *cesado ya la opacidad,* cuando sus propios versos prueban lo contrario.' *El Argos*, 16 June 1821.

39   *An Englishman*, p. 90.

In its first edition of 1823, *El Argos* congratulated the government of Buenos Aires for the accomplishments of the previous year, and for having finally established the values of the European Enlightenment, by way of the wide variety of reforms it put forward, encouraging it to continue doing so:

> Oh, fortunate times! In which the celebrated Plato's maxim began to be fulfilled: people are happy when philosophers govern, or those who govern philosophise. Citizens, do not disappoint our descendants from such glorious hopes. Enlightenment and firmness have marked our steps during the brilliant path in '22. Enlightenment and firmness should be our badge in '23. You have already placed the first stones of the sumptuous social edifice: let the year '23 see you complete it.[40]

This quote reflects the way in which certain sectors of *porteño* society celebrated the efforts of Rivadavia and his group to establish a stronger relationship between the population and the main features of the so-called 'spirit' of the Enlightenment. It was believed that such an aspiration could be achieved through the socio-political reforms sanctioned by the Rodríguez government, and by stimulating diverse cultural and artistic activity to do away with 'anachronistic customs' of the colonial past and establish a new republican order. The chronicles that give an account of evident enthusiasm for civic festivities and artistic activity, especially the theatre, within *porteño* society, confirm that these entertainments effectively spread the ideals that the government was trying to encourage.

However, the nature of the reforms introduced by the Rodríguez government, especially in the religious and military spheres, also provoked a strong reaction and even popular repudiation, which would

---

40 '¡Epoca venturosa! en que empezó a cumplirse la máxima del célebre Platón: los pueblos son felices cuando gobiernan los filósofos, o filosofan los que gobiernan. Ciudadanos, no defraudemos á nuestros descendientes de tan gloriosas esperanzas. La ilustración y la firmeza han distinguido vuestros pasos en la brillante carrera del 22. La ilustración y la firmeza deben ser nuestra divisa en el 23. Habéis colocado ya las primeras piedras del suntuoso edificio social: que el año 23 vea el complemento.' *El Argos*, 1 January 1823.

deepen polarisation in the city. In that same year of 1823 Father Castañeda directed, from his exile in Montevideo, more of his sarcastic and combative criticism at the *porteño* government, aiming to win over those sectors clearly displeased with the mentioned reforms:

> But charity, love and compassion, which are inseparable from my ministry, force me to be advocate and defender of that same province for which I find myself civilly dead. So it is necessary to stay my tears while I commit myself entirely to the defence; and so it is that I do not doubt in assuring to V.H. by what is most sacred, and placing my hand on my heart, under the priest's oath, that I know with a certain precision that our extinction, our civil death, and other insults, are not the work of the Buenos Aires province, but rather the work of some men who do not know what they are doing, and who, while professing a philosophism and Jacobinism, ignoring what Jacobinism and philosophism are, have managed at the expense of the revolution a favourable moment and a fateful hour, which have been theirs, to give a blow to those instincts that are the strongholds of our Holy Faith, and of the celestial dogma, which they abhor and detest not out of malice, but out of the vanity of wanting to emulate Martin Luther and Henry VIII, Frederick II and Bolingbroke, and others who because of their wickedness became highly regarded in this valley of pilgrimages and miseries.[41]

41 'Pero la caridad, amor y compasión inseparable de mi ministerio me obliga a ser abogado y defensor de esa misma provincia para quien me hallo civilmente muerto, preciso es pues, suspender mis lágrimas mientras hago en toda forma la defensa; y así es que no dudo en asegurar a V.H. por lo más sagrado, y con las manos puestas en mi pecho bajo la palabra de sacerdote, que me consta de cierta ciencia que nuestra extinción, nuestra muerte civil y demás afrentas no han sido obra de la provincia bonaerense, sino de unos hombres que no saben lo que se hacen, y que profesando el filosofismo y jacobinismo sin saber lo que es jacobinismo y filosofismo han logrado a expensas de la revolución un momento favorable y una hora aciaga, que ha sido de ellos, para dar como han dado un golpe de mano a esos instintos que son los baluartes de la santa fé, y del dogma celestial, que ellos aborrecen y detestan no por malicia, sino por la vanidad de parecerse a Martín Lutero, a Enrique octavo, a Federico segundo, a Bolimbroque [sic], y a otros que por iniquidad

The tensions generated by increasing antagonism in the city became evident in a few political skirmishes which took place that year, the sharpest occurring in March with the revolt led by Gregorio Tagle against the government in rejection of both the ecclesiastical and military reforms. That episode shows that some sectors of *porteño* society conspicuously failed to identify themselves with the religious reform, the essence of the 'Enlightenment' or the lay spirit prevalent at the time. In his commentary on this particular episode, which took place in March 1823, Juan María Gutiérrez described it as part of a strong socio-cultural cleft that would increasingly divide Buenos Aires society:

> A process with all requisite solemnity showed that those who inspired the revolt were none other than those who disagreed with a situation in which only morality and knowledge could aspire to the public destiny. During that evening a great moral triumph was achieved by the Authority based on the love of justice and the law. It cannot be denied, however, that in the lower and more obscure regions of society the rumour of the protest against the enlightened aspirations of that same authority could be heard, an echo of the past, which in the language of the reformers was called fanaticism.[42]

---

se hicieron respetables en este valle de romerías y miserias.' *Doña María Retazos*, August 1823, pp. 302–3.

For Tagle's attempt at revolt and Castañeda's exile during Rivadavia's government, see Myers, 'Las paradojas de la opinión,' pp. 86–90; and also G. Di Meglio, '¿Una feliz experiencia? La plebe urbana de Buenos Aires y el problema de la legitimidad posrevolucionaria a la luz del "motín de Tagle" (1823),' in *Entrepasados*, year XIV, no. 28 (2005), pp. 103–25.

42 'Un proceso rodeado de todas las solemnidades necesarias puso de manifiesto que los inspiradores de aquella asonada no eran otros que los mal avenidos con una situación en que sólo la moralidad y el saber podían aspirar a los destinos públicos. En aquella noche obtuvo un gran triunfo moral la Autoridad fundada en el amor a la justicia y las leyes. No puede negarse, sin embargo, que en las regiones bajas y obscuras de la sociedad se sentía el rumor de la protesta contra las miras ilustradas de esa misma autoridad, eco del pasado, que en el lenguaje de los reformadores se denominaba fanatismo.' Gutiérrez, *Juan Carlos Varela*, p. 210.

In reference to the same episode, the anonymous Englishman was palpably struck by the participation of what he referred to as hundreds of *gauchos* on horseback who, to the shout of '*Viva la religión*', voiced their clear opposition to the reforms.[43]

These circumstances marked the beginning of the demise of the cultural-ideological atmosphere that had prevailed in Buenos Aires during the previous years. Political disagreements were to increase dramatically during Rivadavia's brief presidency of 1826–27, as a result of the first symptoms of the *unitarios* and *federales* and the outbreak of war with Brazil. In the decades that followed the essence of the 'enlightened' or 'Voltairean' spirit gradually evaporated in *porteño* society, its initial proponents becoming mired in political discord and beset by the factional disputes that would ravage the River Plate scene during the years of the Rosas regime.

---

43   *An Englishman*, p. 234.

In the Eyes of the Albion: The Rise and Fall of Rivadavia as Perceived by British Observers

John Parish Robertson, the Scottish merchant and financier, has been considered, along with his brother William, one of the pioneers of British trade in South America. In a letter of March 1824 sent to his grandfather in Britain, he summarised Rivadavia's role as chief minister of the government of Buenos Aires in the following terms:

> He [Rivadavia] will be recognised as the first man in the revolution who taught his countrymen what true liberty was; and who by a singular combination of prudence, energy, vigour and moderation, united all the discordant elements of anarchy and civil war, and afterwards used them in the very work of regeneration which the political ignorance and profligacy of former systems had made at once so necessary and difficult with all.[1]

This statement seems to reflect the sentiments of many British merchants in Buenos Aires during the 1821–26 period. The commercial and diplomatic ties established by Bernardino Rivadavia with Britain in the early nineteenth century, particularly during the period he was minister of government in Buenos Aires and when he later became Argentina's first president, in many ways represents a starting point of the controversies that abound through the history of the relationship between the two nations.

---

1   Extract of a letter from J.P. Robertson to Mr. Parish of Bath, 10 March 1824. P.R.O., F.O. 6/1. The Robertsons' grandfather was regarded by them as the head of their connection, and occasionally sent the reports of these two brothers to the Foreign Office. For this particular subject, see H.S. Ferns, *Britain and Argentina in the Nineteenth Century* (Oxford, 1960), p. 101.

This subject acquired great intensity half a century ago when certain Argentine historians, particularly those of nationalistic tendencies, and the *revisionista* school agreed that the economic and political dependency of Argentina upon Britain began precisely at that moment.[2] Reading the various accounts of British diplomats, merchants and travellers in Buenos Aires during the 1820s, one is struck by the fact that, in spite of the widespread approval of Rivadavia by many members of the British community in the River Plate, there was also significant criticism of him by other British citizens who resided in those regions, reflecting the complex and sometimes paradoxical features of the *rioplatense*'s liaison with subjects from that nation.[3]

It is also quite revealing that Rivadavia's affinities with his British acquaintances began to fade in 1825, shortly after Britain had formally recognised Argentina's independence from Spain, an objective Rivadavia had been anxiously seeking during his years as a diplomat and politician. The achievement of this diplomatic formality between the two nations had been sealed with the signing of the Treaty of Commerce, Friendship and Navigation that established freedom of commerce between both nations and also freedom of religion for British residents in Argentina.[4] It was important that at this particular juncture Lord Liverpool's government, with George

2   Some examples of this particular stance towards Rivadavia and Britain can be clearly appreciated in works such as J. Irazusta, *Influencia económica británica en el Río de la Plata* (Buenos Aires, 1985); J.M. Rosa, *Rivadavia y el imperialismo financiero* (Buenos Aires, 1964); R. Scalabrini Ortiz, *Política británica en el Río de la Plata* (Buenos Aires, 1940).

3   In his standard work on the relations between these two countries during the nineteenth century Ferns clearly emphasises the constraints involved in many of Rivadavia's dealings with British individuals during the 1820s (*Britain and Argentina*, pp. 131–94).

4   In addition to Fern's book, others that have dealt at length with the process of British recognition of South America and Argentina in particular are: R. Humphreys, *British Consular Reports on the Trade and Politics of Latin America 1824–26* (London, 1952); J. Rydjord, *Foreign Interest in the Independence of New Spain* (Durham NC, 1935); C. Webster, *Britain and the Independence of Latin America 1812–1830*, 2 vols. (London, 1938); Kaufmann, *British Policy*; J. Lynch, 'British Policy and the Independence of Latin America,' in *Journal of Latin American Studies*, no. 1, pp. 1–30 (1969); J. Street, *Gran Bretaña y la independencia del Río de la Plata* (Buenos Aires, 1967); Gallo, *Great Britain and Argentina*.

Canning now acting as foreign secretary, was beginning to break away from the Holy Alliance and seeking to expand its control over transoceanic markets.

The informal diplomatic and commercial relations between Great Britain and the River Plate had not exactly been flourishing up to this stage. The policies applied during Pueyrredón's directorship, between 1816 and 1819, had been regarded by most British residents in the Plate area as unfavourable to their commercial interests. The Pueyrredón government had been reluctant to allow the export of bullion and had unsuccessfully attempted to impose a series of forced loans on the British community; worse followed when the political crisis of 1819–20 produced a marked reduction in commercial activity. Much British merchandise remained unsold for a long time.[5]

Therefore, the reforms introduced by the Rodríguez administration, especially those which made elastic trade regulations more flexible, were welcomed, as can be seen in William Parish Robertson's flattering account of the first two years of Rivadavia's experience as Minister of Government in another letter sent to his grandfather:

> The present Government continues most deservedly to enjoy the entire confidence of the people and I believe it has been truly said that Rivadavia our Minister has done as much *good* as all the others have done *harm* to the country, which is saying a great deal.[6]

Here it is important to note the tariff law of January 1822, which declared taxes on imported merchandise at a basic rate of 15 per cent *ad valorem*. According to Burgin and Bushnell, these measures represented a moderate protectionism for some local products that did not alter significantly a general support for free trade.[7] Also worth mentioning is the decree of Minister of Finance Manuel García in July 1822 prohibiting the sale of public lands and introducing the

5 Lynch, *Spanish American Revolutions*, p. 76.
6 W.P. Robertson to Mr. Parish of Bath, 25 July 1823, P.R.O., F.O. 6/1.
7 M. Burgin, *Aspectos económicos del federalismo argentino* (Buenos Aires, 1969), pp. 105–11; Bushnell, *Reform and Reaction*, p. 129. For a review of the most important economic measures of the governments in which Rivadavia participated, see Bagú, *El plan económico del grupo rivadaviano*.

Emphyteusis Law, a system of long-term leases of public land, and the creation of the Sociedad de Beneficencia in April 1823.

At that time the city of London was experiencing financial turmoil as a consequence of the increased value of South American shares, which eventually led to a series of loans being extended by British banks to a number of the emerging nations in the region.[8] The government of Buenos Aires was, therefore, determined to press harder to obtain recognition of Argentine independence by Great Britain, which eventually extended this early in 1825, leading to the commencement of formal commercial and diplomatic relations between the two nations.[9]

The favourable remarks made by British diplomatic agents and a range of British residents about the Buenos Aires ministry prompted Canning to send to Buenos Aires one of the three consuls selected as diplomatic representatives in the newly formed Latin American states. The other two countries chosen for the commencement of formal diplomatic relations with Britain were New Granada and Mexico. The envoy selected to occupy the post in the River Plate, Woodbine Parish, happened to be a relative of the Robertson brothers.

Shortly after arriving in Buenos Aires in March 1824, the new British Consul was informed that Rivadavia 'had done more for the general amelioration of this state in the last three years than all his predecessors in power'.[10] However, Woodbine Parish's early accounts also expressed a certain anxiety about the uncertain political prospects, now that the Rodríguez administration was to be replaced by a newly elected one:

> Upon the whole, whatever may be its result, what has passed upon has had an almost excellent effect: the spontaneous expression of so public a feeling with respect to M. Rivadavia's administration, is the best proof which can be given of the general and great anxiety felt here, for the continuance, and preservation of that system which has

8   On this subject, see F.G. Dawson, *The First Latin American Debt Crisis: The City of London and the 1822–1825 Loan Bubble* (New Haven, 1990).
9   Gallo, *Great Britain and Argentina*, pp. 115–60.
10   W. Parish to G. Canning, 27 April 1824, P.R.O., F.O. 6/3.

been so benefited to every real interest in this country, and the best assurance to M. Rivadavia's successor, whoever he may be, that he will receive every necessary support in following the same good course.[11]

The new governor, General Las Heras, referred to the previous government as '*la feliz experiencia*', and certainly did aspire to the 'preservation of the system' by attempting to follow the course of his predecessor.[12] However, shortly after assuming power, representatives of the River Plate provinces were already debating in a constituent assembly how to bring about national reunification, a precondition imposed by the British for their acceptance of independence and the fulfilment of the commercial agreement.

What had impressed many British observers about the Rodríguez government was the fact that, unlike those of the first decade, it was to be one of the first since independence to contain a considerable number of politicians of both civilian and clerical origin, many of whom would play significant roles either as ministers or legislators. Such were the cases of Ignacio Nuñez and Manuel García, and the clerics Julián Segundo de Agüero and Valentín Gómez. There were also well-known personalities in the opposition groups, whose attacks focused on the centralist tendency adopted by the government. Manuel Dorrego, the eccentric Father Castañeda and Manuel Moreno, brother of Mariano, one of the most charismatic leaders of the 1810 revolution, were some of the most prominent members of these factions.

Despite the antagonisms that existed between government and opposition — which one of the Robertson brothers would describe rather casually as 'Whig and Tory' — for most British observers an atmosphere of mutual respect and political harmony had essentially prevailed. One example of this congenial political climate was the support given to the government by the majority of the opposition when Tagle — a former member of the Pueyrredón administration who headed the military officers opposed to the reform of November 1821 that established a large decrease in the size of the army — conspired twice to bring down Rodríguez by a military coup.

11   W. Parish to G. Canning, 27 April 1824, P.R.O., F.O. 6/3.
12   L.A. Romero, *La feliz experiencia 1820–1824* (Buenos Aires, 1976), p. 7.

That support seemed to confirm the early optimism expressed by the United States Commercial Agent John Murray Forbes in relation to Rivadavia's political capacity. As early as September 1821 he referred to the Buenos Aires Minister of Government as 'father of this incipient system of order and virtue' and as an indispensable figure for the prevalence of civilian influence over that of the military.[13] However, the American diplomat considered that certain members of the opposition factions, notably Manuel Moreno ('a friend of our nation'), were more devoted to the United States.[14] Forbes's praise of Rivadavia's talents were shared by the anonymous Englishman (who was, according to some historians, George Love, the founder of *The British Packet*, a *porteño* weekly) who described the government of Rodríguez as 'excellent', also attributing its success to Rivadavia's skills.[15] Similarly, Woodbine Parish was duly impressed by the style of deliberations that took place in the new assembly:

> The proceedings of the 'Sala' are open to the public, and are conducted with the greatest propriety and order, the building in which the assembly meets is arranged some what after the manner of the chamber of deputies in Paris, the seats of the members being laid out in the form of a semi lane, in the centre and front of which is placed the tribune appropriated to the President and secretaries.[16]

The government's attempts to achieve the Benthamite goal of establishing a harmonious civil society in *porteño* society via public deliberation, transparency and the wide diffusion of information was viewed with mixed feelings by the British residents. The Rivadavian custom of accountability to the *porteño* population, for instance, seemed to irritate Woodbine Parish, who complained about this practice. The British diplomat was perplexed as to why Rivadavia had decided to translate and publish in *El Argos* a copy of an official dispatch sent to him by Canning:

13   J.M. Forbes to J.Q. Adams, 11 September 1821, quoted in Forbes, *Once años*, p. 137.
14   J.M. Forbes to J.Q. Adams, 29 August 1822, in *Once años*, p. 198.
15   *An Englishman*, p. 155.
16   W. Parish to G. Canning, 17 May 1824, P.R.O., F.O. 6/3.

I did not hesitate to express to M. Rivadavia my feelings upon
this subject and how much I regretted that he should have
given publicity in such manner to such a document, and how
much inconvenience might be occasioned if all the commu-
nications we were to hold in future were to be so abruptly laid
upon to the general observation, that I had only to hope it
would not be productive in this instance of inconvenience,
and that on any other occasion he would at least have the
goodness to apprise me of any similar intentions.[17]

Although he eventually apologised, Rivadavia could not avoid
defending his action as justifiable and unavoidable:

M. Rivadavia expressed his regret that he had taken any
step which I could think might possibly lead to inconvenience, but pleaded the general custom of this government
to send to the newspaper any documents of general importance, and that it was impossible for him to lay before the
public one of greater interest than this.[18]

These misunderstandings aside, Parish was disappointed that
Rivadavia had decided not to accept General Las Heras's invitation
to join his government:

It was with very considerable regret that I learnt from him
[Rivadavia] in reply to my enquiries that he had made up
his mind to withdraw from his official situation: He
entered upon the subject with me confidentially and unre-
servedly. He stated that the plan of the triennial change of
government had been his own, and he would not suffer it
to be said he himself would be the first to deviate from it.
He considered that by his personally retiring at this
moment and allowing the constitutional cause to take
effect, he strengthened rather than weakened the
Government. He was convinced, he said, that all those that
had any property at stake and all thinking men would continue to support his measures. He knew that he had creat-

17   W. Parish to G. Canning, 7 April 1824, P.R.O., F.O. 6/3.
18   *Ibid.*

ed some personal enemies by steps he had been obliged to take in the course of the last three years: but general benefit has accrued and it was the man rather than the measures to which even his enemies had now a dislike. By his own personal retirement, he felt he was removing the only objection which could be made to them. Mr. Rivadavia entered at great length into his feelings upon this subject, the principal drift of which was to prove to me that he acted from a conviction that by adhering to the line laid down by the constitution of the State, he should morally strengthen the present form of Government in the public opinion. To all this I could only reply by expressing how much I must regret, after the personal explanations we had had together, that the time was so soon to come when I was to lose the benefit of his official assistance. [19]

Although Parish appreciated the skills of the new minister, Manuel García, he considered that person not to have 'the same energy, [and] strength of mind, which has characterised Mr. Rivadavia'.[20] A great proportion of the British community in Buenos Aires was equally satisfied with Rivadavia's administration during his three years as minister. The fact that the anonymous Englishman referred to him as 'the William Pitt of Buenos Aires' is clear evidence of the esteem he enjoyed amongst this group of immigrants that consisted mainly of merchants.[21] According to the same author, by 1822 there were 3,500 British residents in Buenos Aires — Woodbine Parish estimated 3,000 — who he considered dominated the economy of the city.[22] This was not an entirely exaggerated notion if one bears in mind the large amount of land acquired by British investors during that time. It was also common knowledge that most of the directors of the Banco de Descuentos, created in June 1822, were British, and that there were almost 40 British commercial establishments operating in the city. Equally important in this respect was that half of the public debt of

19   W. Parish to G. Canning, 27 April 1824, P.R.O., F.O. 6/3.
20   W. Parish to G. Canning, 19 February 1825, P.R.O., F.O. 6/8.
21   *An Englishman*, p. 155.
22   *Ibid.*, p. 45; Humphreys, *British Consular Reports*, p. 26.

the Province of Buenos Aires was said to be in British hands.[23] Annual imports from Britain were valued at US$5,730,952, against US$1,368,277 from the United States and US$820,109 from France.[24]

The predominance of British interests in Buenos Aires was particularly resented by most of the North Americans residing in that city. Forbes sadly admitted to his Secretary of State, John Quincy Adams, that in spite of his nation's efforts to spread 'moral prestige' in the River Plate, the British, thanks to their commercial superiority, had managed to exercise a higher degree of influence over *porteño* society.[25] Particularly disturbing for Forbes was the fact that the Monroe Doctrine was given almost no importance in the River Plate Provinces, whereas British recognition of their independence had been anxiously awaited.[26]

Shortly after leaving the government in mid-1824, Rivadavia again set sail to England with the purpose of visiting his two sons studying there.[27] Parish and Canning trusted that his trip would also have diplomatic consequences, and that it would advance the recognition question and the prospects for the reunification of the Argentine provinces.[28] Although these expectations were to prove justified, it was at this stage that their positive image of Rivadavia began to change.

Recognition, War and Presidency

The Anglo-Argentine Treaty of Commerce, Navigation and Friendship was signed whilst Rivadavia was still in the United Kingdom. Canning managed to persuade a majority of the members of the Liverpool cabinet to recognise Argentina as an independent nation. This declaration was achieved despite the opposition of diehard Tories such as the Duke of Wellington, and in the face of the

23   Ferns, *Britain and Argentina*, p. 101.
24   Dawson, *The First Latin American Debt Crisis*, p. 79.
25   J.M. Forbes to J.Q. Adams, 3 January 1823, published in Forbes, *Once años*, p. 214.
26   *An Englishman*, p. 61.
27   Williford, *Jeremy Bentham on Spanish America*, p. 103.
28   W. Parish to G. Canning, 20 June 1824, and G. Canning to W. Parish, 29 September 1824, P.R.O., F.O. 6/7.

reluctance of George IV, who was equally suspicious and prejudiced about the new South American republics.

Woodbine Parish had played an important role in British recognition by providing Canning with evidence that the South American nation was on its way towards consolidating internal political stability and securing national reunification. The request for that intelligence was met thanks to Parish's confidence in Manuel García's assurances that the Constituent Assembly would decree the unification of the Argentine provinces in the near future.[29] A few months before that agreement was reached, Canning had bitterly complained to Parish about Rivadavia's conduct during his stay in London:

> M. Rivadavia lived while here, in constant intercourse with commercial establishments in this country, establishments highly respectable but still consisting of persons deeply interested in the fluctuation of commercial affairs. I desire that you will lose no opportunity of impressing upon M. Garcia how inexpedient it is that the Gov. of Buenos Ayres should place the conduct of their affairs in the hands of any person in such a situation.[30]

The British foreign minister had already expressed his anger to Parish a few months before, when he made reference of Rivadavia's double diplomatic mission to Britain and France, which Canning had not expected and considered intolerable. Rivadavia's financial dealings with Hullett & Company he also considered most inappropriate. Parish duly transmitted these irregularities of Rivadavia's proceedings to García, who in turn attempted to justify the former minister's behaviour:

> I afterwards entered at some length with M. García upon that part of your dispatch which relates to M. de Rivadavia having lived so much with commercial men in England and the obvious inconveniences arising from a political agent giving himself up to such connections: In the justness and pro-

29   Ferns, *Britain and Argentina*, pp. 109–30. Gallo, *De la invasión al reconocimiento*, pp. 203–37.

30   G. Canning to W. Parish, 26 September 1825, P.R.O., F.O. 6/7. Also published in Webster, *Britain and the Independence of Latin America*, vol. 1, pp. 127–9.

priety of this principle, M. García could not but most entirely concur, but he observed that it was due to M. de Rivadavia
to say that in his particular case such connections had entirely arisen out of the peculiar situation in which he stood during his stay in England: that he went hither as a private
individual with the object of promoting the establishment of
very useful institutions and projects for his own country, in
furthermore of which pursuit he fell necessarily into the
hands of the individuals engaged in commercial pursuits, and
amongst such connections as it will perhaps have been difficult for him during the remainder of his short stay in
England to have easily thrown off.[31]

It was also during this trip that Rivadavia's friendship with Bentham
was to come to an abrupt end. Shortly after the South American's
departure from England, Bentham wrote in critical terms about his
personality to none other than Simón Bolívar, although he still
seemed eager to seek more information about the political developments in the region:

> As to Rivadavia, though there is something in his disposi-
> tion that does not chime with the sociableness of mine,
> yet from what I have seen of him, added to what every-
> body knows of him, I cannot but believe that if your
> agents, whoever they are, are qualified to make the obser-
> vation, your commonwealths might derive considerable
> information by their noting and reporting to you what is
> going forward there [in Buenos Aires].[32]

The English philosopher was surely unaware of the extent to which
Rivadavia disliked the Venezuelan liberator. It was Woodbine Parish
who felt it necessary to communicate to Canning his utter disgust at
Rivadavia's insinuations about Bolívar's despotic political tendencies:

> Notwithstanding sundry symptoms of jealousy which I
> have occasionally noticed in the government of Buenos
> Ayres of the preeminent reputation of General Bolívar, I

31 W. Parish to G. Canning, 15 December 1825, P.R.O., F.O. 6/8
32 J. Bentham to S. Bolívar, 13 August 1825, UCL, Box XII.

was much surprised at the extent to which M. Rivadavia on this occasion thought proper to give vent to the expression of such feelings — feelings I confess, and I regret to say so, which I am much more inclined to attribute to personal than political motives.[33]

Bentham was to remain puzzled by Rivadavia's sudden decision to ignore him, and he was convinced that this had to do with the fact that the latter was dealing with members of the Tory government, who scarcely appreciated the philosopher's political principles. Nevertheless, Jonathan Harris has stated that Rivadavia was worried that the British government might not concede recognition to Argentina because of his dealings with the Hullett firm, of which Bentham was also an associate. According to this author, it was the philosopher's connection with that firm that motivated Rivadavia's decision to avoid contacting him.[34]

The negotiations between Rivadavia and Hullett & Company were mostly related to the mines of Famatina in the province of La Rioja that allegedly contained gold and silver. Rivadavia had alerted Hullett to the apparent potential of these mines in 1823 and, during his trip to London, persuaded the firm to invest one million pounds in the venture by creating the Río de la Plata Mining Company. However, a series of clashes with other British and Argentine investors who created a rival company, organised for the same purpose by the Robertson brothers, and the unfavourable reports on the condition of the Famatina mine written by Francis Bond Head, sent there by the directors of the Río de la Plata Mining Company, precipitated the collapse of the enterprise.[35]

The other venture that would cloud future entanglements and with which Rivadavia was involved whilst in London was the Baring Brothers' loan of a million pounds to the government of Buenos Aires that became effective in July 1824. This loan had been sought by Rivadavia whilst acting as minister, and had been approved by the

33   W. Parish to G. Canning, 21 April 1826, P.R.O., F.O. 6/11
34   Harris, 'Bernardino Rivadavia and Benthamite Discipleship,' pp. 149–55.
35   Ferns, *Britain and Argentina*, pp. 134–7; F.B. Head, *Reports Relating to the Failure of the Rio Plata Mining Association* (London, 1827).

assembly in August 1822. The money was supposed to be used by the *porteño* government to build port facilities, to provide the city with running water and to build towns in the southern frontier in order to discourage Indian raids, but it ended up being mostly invested in the Argentine–Brazilian war which broke out shortly afterwards.[36]

National unification in the River Plate was finally achieved in February 1826 and Rivadavia was elected as its president, but only after two years of deliberations amongst the representatives of the different provinces. In his meeting with the new president, Woodbine Parish sensed a marked change in his attitude:

> The extreme formality with which M. de Rivadavia received me was so strikingly different from the frank and cordial manner, which had given me so much satisfaction on all former public occasions in this country, that I should have been inclined to consider it as having been purposely intended, had I not afterwards learnt that the North American Chargé d'Affaires met a like stiff reception, and was equally surprised by it.[37]

From this point onwards, the tenor of Woodbine Parish's criticism towards Rivadavia's policies and attitudes as president would increase. The British diplomat acutely foresaw in the very early stages of this presidency the problems that would surely lie ahead if Rivadavia was to persist with this attitude:

> Had M. Rivadavia proceeded with a very moderate degree of circumspection, and attention to those local feelings, and institutions, which have now for some years been so studiously respected by his predecessors, he would have found little difficulty in carrying all his wishes with the

---

36 Ferns, *Britain and Argentina*, 141–7; Dawson, *The First Latin American Debt Crisis*, pp. 77–80. Also on this subject, S. Amaral, 'El Empréstito de Londres de 1824,' in *Desarrollo económico*, vol. 23, no. 92, enero–marzo 1984; E.J. Fitte, *Historia de un Empréstito: La emisión de Baring Brothers en 1824* (Buenos Aires, 1962); H. Galmarini, *Los negocios del poder: Reforma y crisis del estado 1776/1826* (Buenos Aires, 2000), pp. 251–312.

37 W. Parish to G. Canning, 12 February 1826, P.R.O., F.O. 6/11.

> Buenos Ayreans, and in convincing them of the real advan-
> tages of his project to their own interests, but instead of this,
> he has adopted a violent course which makes him at once
> unpopular here, and will I fear give rise to such a systematic
> spirit of opposition to his measures in the other provinces, as
> will be productive of the greatest embarrassments.[38]

Almost inevitably Woodbine Parish began to place his confidence
more and more in García, whom he now regarded as 'one of the best
and most enlightened' politicians he had met in Buenos Aires.[39] This
statesman had not joined Rivadavia's government, largely due to his
disagreements with Julián Segundo de Agüero, the minister of government, as well as with the president himself. García was also
becoming the most favoured political personality amongst other
British diplomats and merchants in the River Plate.

Another British visitor who suffered from the attitude of the new
head of state was John Beaumont, who arrived in the River Plate in
order to supervise the fate of British colonists who had encountered
all sorts of difficulty since arriving there. These immigrants were
part of an agricultural colonisation project that had been created by
Rivadavia and Beaumont's father during the *rioplatense*'s diplomatic
mission in Europe of 1814–20. Rivadavia's pompous and dismissive
reaction towards the problems surrounding this enterprise incensed
Beaumont and led him on to write a most negative account about
him in his well-known book of his travels in Argentina.[40]

Immediately after assuming power, Rivadavia was to encounter a
complicated situation on both the internal and external fronts. The
clear centralist tendency of his government, supported by the *unitario*
faction, was the main cause of opposition in a number of provinces,
some of which had decided not to accept the 1826 Constitution that

38   W. Parish to G. Canning, 14 March 1826, P.R.O. F.O. 6/11.
39   W. Parish to G. Canning, 20 July 1826, P.R.O., F.O. 6/11.
40   J.A.B. Beaumont, *Viajes por Buenos Aires, Entre Ríos y la Banda Oriental
     (1826–1827)* (Buenos Aires, 1957), pp. 187–90 (Original title: *Travels in Buenos
     Ayres and the Adjacent Provinces of the Rio de la Plata, Intended for the use of Persons
     who Contemplate Emigrating to that Country or Embarking Capital in its Affairs*
     (London, 1828); Ferns, *Britain and Argentina*, pp. 137–43.

promulgated national reunification and a centralist presidency. The
province of Córdoba, led by an old enemy of Rivadavia, the *caudillo*
Juan Bautista Bustos, was heading the *federalista* cause in the interior
against the government. More worrying still was the outbreak of war
with Brazil in late 1825. The Portuguese presence in the Banda
Oriental had always been of great concern for the River Plate governments, and was even more so after Brazilian independence was
declared and Uruguay was incorporated into the new empire as the
Cisplatine Province of Brazil. When a group of Uruguayan rebels
landed in Buenos Aires in April 1825 to demand the inclusion of
their territory in the River Plate Provinces — a petition that the
Buenos Aires government duly accepted — Brazil immediately
declared war on Argentina.

This crisis seriously affected British commercial interests in the
area as a consequence of the Brazilian navy's decision to blockade
the Río de la Plata estuary. The fact that both nations were important
trading partners of Great Britain in South America precipitated
Canning's decision to mediate as soon as possible. The intervention
of the British government in this conflict was much desired by
Rivadavia, who stressed to Parish that British intervention was vital:

> The consequences of the war, he [Rivadavia] said, were
> daily becoming more embarrassing to this Government,
> and he could not say into what a state of disorganisation it
> was likely to throw the whole country, especially the interi-
> or provinces, if it continued much longer; but that, consid-
> ering the personal character of the Emperor of Brazil, he
> saw no means of terminating it at hand except by the inter-
> vention of Great Britain, as a friendly power, and with, as
> he could not but suppose from recent circumstances, a par-
> ticular influence over the Councils of his Imperial Majesty
> which no other Government could urge with the same jus-
> tice and force.[41]

Canning sent Lord John Ponsonby as British Minister to Buenos
Aires, hoping that mediation would be made easier by the supposed

41   W. Parish to G. Canning, 21 April 1826, P.R.O., F.O. 6/11

willingness of Rivadavia's government to reach peace. Ponsonby, who, rumour had it, attracted the attention of Lady Connyngham, George IV's favourite, arrived in Buenos Aires in September 1826.[42] By the following month he was bitterly complaining to Canning about Rivadavia's political and economic blunders:

> He [Rivadavia] fostered and gave activity to the wild and foolish spirit of the mob, to which this most disastrous war owes its true origin. He neglected (when engaged in the war) to provide whilst it was yet possible to provide, for the carrying it on with effect, that is, while the river was still open. He has since directed the exertions of the Government to operations on land, not seeing that it was by naval means alone that he could ward off the fatal blow aimed at the state, and the only fatal blow that could be aimed at it, by Brazil. He has supported the war by recurrence to a paper monetary system of the worst nature (which already threatens to break up in his hands), having previously in London by an act of folly taken the money business of this country out of the hands of Alexander Baring and placed it in the hands of Messrs. Hullett & Co., from whom he can receive no help in his utmost need.[43]

In reference to this letter Halperín has identified Ponsonby's mention of Rivadavia's control of a mob as a curiosity, given the fact that he has usually been identified with an elite insensitive to popular demands.[44] In February 1826, when the Argentine army was winning a succession of victories by land and sea, Ponsonby appeared more concerned with the confrontations between *unitarios* and *federales* in the interior because of what he saw as an imminent invasion of Buenos Aires by the *montoneros* from the provinces.[45]

Although Ponsonby admitted that Rivadavia had in the past been responsible for reforms that were beneficial for British interests, sus-

---

42   Ferns, *Britain and Argentina*, p. 169.
43   J. Ponsonby to G. Canning, 20 October 1826, P.R.O., F.O. 6/13; also quoted in Webster, *Britain and the Independence of Latin America*, pp. 156–8.
44   Halperín Donghi, *Historia argentina*, p. 237.
45   J. Ponsonby to G. Canning, 6 February 1827, P.R.O., F.O. 6/16.

picious as he was of republics, let alone utilitarian-inspired policies, he considered that the chaotic political scene that had developed was inevitable. Ponsonby believed that the president's ineptitude was most clearly reflected in dealings with the leading *caudillos* of the provinces, whom the government referred to as 'anarchists', and was a result of 'the total want of any idea of *value of law*, and the rooted habits of insubordination amongst the people'.[46] A few months later it became evident that he had almost lost all hope in the capacity of Rivadavia's government to control this conflict:

> Sr. Rivadavia, a man of whom I can say nothing good either as a statesman or as the head of a government, beyond the praise that might be due to a bustling mayor of a small town, was, notwithstanding the feeble means desired from his understanding, and the narrow cultivation of it, unfortunately dominated by a furious ambition; to this passion he was ready to sacrifice his country, and to it he did sacrifice his own power seeking to augment it beyond right, and without any reasonable chance of success. In the madness of this passion he imagined himself to be the rival of Mr. Canning, and when he was falling from power, in consequence of his own manifold errors in politics and his want of manners (so powerfully operative even in the affairs of Empires) he was pleased to direct himself with redoubled wrath and venom against what he supposed to be English interests here, and chiefly against myself, who he imagined to be most vulnerable by his blows. He let loose slander against England and against me.[47]

A more favourable and comprehensive British description of Rivadavia's presidency, a couple of years after the latter's downfall, was provided by General William Miller, General San Martín's aide-de-camp, to none other than Jeremy Bentham, who by then had probably lost his former enthusiasm for the fate of Argentina and, for that matter, Rivadavia:

---

46 J. Ponsonby to G. Canning, 9 March 1827, P.R.O., F.O. 6/17
47 J. Ponsonby to G. Canning, 20 July 1827, P.R.O., F.O. 6/18

The system which had worked so well before was discarded, and the spirit of innovation substituted the 'one and indivisible', or as they call it the 'central form' of government; but *Gaucho* sense would not tolerate the measure which deprived them of a positive good, nor *Gaucho* pride brook the change which conferred on Buenos Ayres a palpable supremacy. Division arose and the provinces severely withdrew from the federation. We have seen that fine portion of America retrograding from bad to worse, until it has become a question, whether a war of colour will be the fatal consequence of Rivadavia's error, where this horrid state of things is to end, is difficult to foresee; but it appears certain to my mind that Buenos Ayres might slowly restore the provinces to the federal bond by the re-establishment of a good government; but that she will never be able to conquer them by force of arms. Nor, indeed ought she to wish it; for provincial jealousies and petty feuds cannot deprive her of the metropolitan precedency, which geography assigns to her, in the Argentine territories, and which might render her an emporium, like that Venice was in former days.[48]

The hugely unpopular and controversial peace accord signed with the Brazilian Empire in June 1827 by García — who in spite of his antagonism towards the president was sent to Rio de Janeiro as a diplomatic envoy — marked the virtual end of Rivadavia's government. The agreement consisted of a series of measures in favour of Brazil, which were only modified later when independence was granted to Uruguay. Rivadavia vehemently denounced the terms of García's treaty with the Brazilians, but was beset with too many political and economic problems at home. Most of the interior provinces were determined to persist in their opposition, and the war with Brazil had left the finances of the nation in a wretched state.[49]

48 W. Miller to J. Bentham, 27 June 1829, letter published in Bowring, *Works of Jeremy Bentham*, vol. 11, p. 16.
49 Ferns, *Britain and Argentina*, pp. 155–84; Halperín Donghi, *Historia argentina*, pp. 235–40.

Ponsonby was at pains to defend García from the anger of most of the *rioplatense* population, and was beginning to pay attention to an increasingly charismatic character to whom Rivadavia had recently given command of the militia of the province of Buenos Aires. The English diplomat described this new commander as 'a man of great activity and extreme popularity amongst the class of the gauchos to which he may almost be said to belong'.[50] He was aware, though, that Rivadavia did not particularly like him: 'Rosas was treated ill by Rivadavia and is his most bitter enemy', and even predicted that this man was destined to play a decisive role in the future.[51]

As noted at the start of this chapter, Argentine historians of the mid-twentieth century, particularly the *Revisionistas*, established a series of distinctions between the political experiences in power of Rivadavia and Rosas. They viewed Rosas's experience as governor of Buenos Aires, 1829–32 and 1835–52, as a parenthesis in the process of political and economic subordination of Argentina to Britain, a position fortified by the fact that Rosas's government suffered the Anglo-French blockade during 1845–48. According to this view, the Rivadavia era, like the governments of the second half of the nineteenth century, stood in stark contrast to the period dominated by Rosas.

In his biography of Juan Manuel de Rosas, John Lynch says that most British diplomats residing in the province of Buenos Aires had supported Rosas's mandates as governor of that region, and had clearly preferred him to other previous Argentine rulers. Among these representatives he included Woodbine Parish, who considered Rosas to be a true 'pacifier' and a more able and effective leader than Rivadavia.[52] Lynch's assessment on this particular matter may not be absolutely novel, but it does in certain ways contradict those Argentine historians who have attempted to emphasise a clear distinction in relation to Rivadavia's and Rosas's attitudes towards Great Britain. At most, from the evidence gathered in the present work, it does not seem exaggerated to support the idea that Rivadavia's liaison with Great Britain was both complex and ambiguous.

50   J. Ponsonby to G. Canning, 20 July 1827, P.R.O., F.O. 6/18.
51   *Ibid.*
52   J. Lynch, *Juan Manuel de Rosas* (Buenos Aires, 1986), p. 250 (Original title: *Argentine Dictator: Juan Manuel de Rosas, 1829–1852*, London, 1981).

Epilogue

On July 1827 Bernardino Rivadavia resigned as president of the United Provinces of the River Plate. Towards the end of that year Argentina returned to a confederate status, a solution that did not reduce the high tensions that prevailed between Buenos Aires and the provinces in the midst of the *federales* and *unitarios* rivalry. A year later, the new governor of Buenos Aires, Manuel Dorrego, aligned with the former group, was ousted and eventually executed without trial by the forces led by *unitario* leader Juan Lavalle, who in turn took over as governor. Although Rivadavia had remained distant from these tragic events, he and many of his friends had decidedly supported Lavalle.

When, in mid-1829, Juan Manuel de Rosas displaced Lavalle from power, Rivadavia and his former political associates, such as Julián Segundo de Agüero, Valentín Gómez, Salvador María del Carril and Juan Cruz Varela among others, were considered as being directly responsible for Dorrego's execution. These men were left with the inevitable alternative of fleeing the country as soon as possible. Rivadavia decided to sail to France and departed from Buenos Aires on May 1829. He remained in Paris until mid-1834, when he returned to Buenos Aires; shortly after he arrived in that city Rosas, who although not yet back in power had acquired by then a tremendous level of influence over the current government of Buenos Aires, suggested that Rivadavia should be forced to leave for Uruguay. In that country he established himself in Colonia until 1836, when he was arrested by order of President Manuel Oribe, an ally of Rosas, who accused Rivadavia and other *unitario* exiles of supporting his main political rival, Fructuoso Rivera.

After two years in detention at the Isla Santa Catalina, Rivadavia and his family were released and shortly afterwards, in late 1839, decided to leave for Rio de Janeiro. In that city, his tribulations did not cease as his wife Juana died there in late 1841. A year later

Rivadavia decided to leave Rio with his three sons, and headed for Spain in order to reside in Cádiz, close to his ancestral home town, where he eventually died on 2 September 1845 at 65 years of age.

The years that followed the downfall of Rivadavia's presidency were not only notable for the internal political antagonisms that continued until the Rosas government fell in 1852, but also had effects on the evolution of political and cultural life in Buenos Aires. Under Rosas the republican system prevailed although both the authoritarian and populist rhetoric and the *unanimista* structure appear as the most distinctive features of that experience in comparison with the 1820s. It is interesting to note, however, that during the Rosista period certain political and cultural practices that had intensified during the *feliz experiencia*, such as elections, widespread diffusion of publicity and political organisation of civic festivities, persisted. It was also possible to observe a development of certain areas of popular culture that had advanced during the 1820s, as is the case of the theatre.[1] It was essentially the adoption of more rigid guidelines for the purpose of imposing order in a turbulent political environment that marked the most significant contrast between the Rivadavian and Rosas eras.

The legacy of Rivadavia's political and intellectual reforms is closely associated with the emergence of the so-called 'romantics' or members of the *Generación del 37* — the young publicists, literary authors and eventual politicians of the post-Rosas years who spent most of that time in exile as a result of their opposition towards his regime. Amongst those most closely associated with the *feliz experiencia* cultural entourage were the Varela brothers, Juan Cruz and Florencio, who were instrumental in guiding and assisting the first literary activities of Sarmiento, Echeverría and Gutiérrez in Montevideo. In many ways the 'Rivadavian experience' had a profound effect on both the literary and political formation of most of the main referents of the *Generación del 37*. In his emblematic *Facundo*, for instance, Sarmiento described with some irony the essence behind the Rivadavian project:

1   On this topic the following works are essential: J. Myers, *Orden y virtud: El discurso republicano en el régimen rosista* (Buenos Aires, 1995); Lacasa, 'Celebrar la *"feliz experiencia"*'; Ternavasio, *La revolución del voto*; Castagnino, *El teatro en Buenos Aires durante la época de Rosas*; M. Rodríguez, 'Rosas y el teatro rioplatense (1835–1852),' in Batticuore, Gallo and Myers (eds.), *Resonancias románticas*, pp. 167–80.

Rivadavia comes from Europe, he brings Europe with him; moreover, he despises Europe; Buenos Aires and, of course, the Argentine Republic would achieve what republican France has not, what the English aristocracy does not want, what despotised Europe misses. This was not Rivadavia's illusion, it was the general thought of the city [Buenos Aires], it was its spirit and tendency.[2]

And Echeverría, author of the *Dogma socialista*, almost obsessively identified the electoral law of 1821 as the turning point of the *feliz experiencia*, practically paving the way for the emergence of Rosas to power:

We had reasons for saying this. The *Unitario* party did not posses local rules of socialist criteria; they dismissed the democratic element: they searched for it in the cities, it was in the countryside. They did not know how to organise it, and for the same reason they did not know how to govern it. Missing this basis, their social edifice would crumble, and it effectively crumbled. They established universal suffrage in order to govern: but in their sufficiency and their aristocratic outbursts, they appeared to or believed they would be able to govern the people; and they lost it and lost the country with all the best intentions.[3]

---

2 'Rivadavia viene de Europa, se trae a la Europa; más todavía, desprecia a la Europa; Buenos Aires, y, por supuesto, decían, la República Argentina, realizará lo que la Francia republicana no ha podido, lo que la aristocracia inglesa no quiere, lo que la Europa despotizada echa de menos. Esto no era una ilusión de Rivadavia, era el pensamiento general de la *ciudad*, era su espíritu y su tendencia.' Sarmiento, *Facundo*, p. 299.

3 'Tuvimos razón para decirlo. El partido unitario no tenía *reglas locales de criterio socialistas*; desconoció el elemento democrático: lo buscó en las ciudades, estaba en las campañas. No supo organizarlo, y por lo mismo no supo gobernarlo. Faltándole esa base, todo su edificio social debió desplomarse, y se desplomó. Estableció el sufragio universal para gobernar en forma por él: pero, en su suficiencia y en sus arranques aristocráticos, aparentó o creyó poder gobernar por el pueblo; y se perdió y perdió al país con la mayor buena fe del mundo.' In 'Ojeada retrospectiva sobre el movimiento intelectual en el Plata desde el año 1837,' in *Esteban Echeverría: Antología de prosa y verso* (Buenos Aires, 1981), p. 149.

The same critical approach, though more moderate in tone, can be perceived in passages of Alberdi's *Bases* describing the Rivadavian period:

> Mister Rivadavia, head of the *Unitario* party of that time, brought over from France and England his enthusiasm and admiration for the system of government he had seen executed with so much success in those ancient states. But neither he nor his supporters realised what conditions were necessary for the existence of centralism in Europe and the obstacles for its application in the Plata. The motives they invoked for its admission, were precisely the ones that made such thing impossible: these being the great extensions of territory, the lack of population, the lack of enlightenment and of resources.[4]

Juan María Gutiérrez was probably the most benevolent of the *Generación del 37* authors with the Rivadavian project. Gutiérrez, who wrote one of the most comprehensive studies on the origins and development of higher education in Buenos Aires as well as a short biography on Rivadavia, considered that:

> Mr. Rivadavia's principal glory consists therefore in having elevated morals in the region of power as basis for his strength and endurance, and in comprehending that the people's education is the fundamental element of happiness and growth. Upon these pillars he founded an administration that has not yet been rivalled in these countries, and part of its creations, like luminous spots, [they] have

---

4   'El señor Rivadavia, jefe del partido unitario de esa época, trajo de Francia y de Inglaterra el entusiasmo y la admiración del sistema de gobierno que había visto en ejercicio con tanto éxito en esos viejos estados. Pero ni él ni sus sectarios se daban cuenta de las condiciones a que debía su existencia el centralismo en Europa y de los obstáculos para su aplicación en el Plata. Los motivos que ellos invocaban en favor de su admisión, son precisamente los que lo hacían imposible: tales eran la grande extensión del territorio, la falta de población, la falta de luces, de recursos.' In Alberdi, *Bases y puntos de partida para la organización política de la república argentina*, passage quoted in Oscar Terán (comp.) *Escritos de Juan Bautista Alberdi. El Redactor de la Ley*, (Buenos Aires, 1996), p. 149.

shone even in the darkest hours of the barbaric government that managed to detain for so many years the march of Argentine progress.[5]

It is probable that Rivadavia placed too much faith in the supposed rationality of his reforms, as Gutiérrez implies, and as indicated by Sarmiento's assumption that his government was based on the philosophy of eighteenth-century European Enlightenment which the governments of early nineteenth century Europe did not dare apply. On the other hand, the implication of the critiques of Rivadavia by both Echeverría and Alberdi indicate that the main problem was a lack of empathy or inability of the Rivadavian group to grasp the diverse spectrum of values and traditions — what Guizot and the *Doctrinaires* commonly referred to as *les mœurs* — that were unfolding in *porteño* and *rioplatense* society and that went beyond the spheres of politics and high culture.

The end of this era was mainly brought about by Rivadavia's lack of ability, and that of his loyal ministers, to deal with the complexities of local and foreign politics at a national level. The complications implicit in the reunification of the country, the war with the Brazilian Empire, the growing antagonisms between *unitarios* and *federales*, together with Rivadavia's own questionable financial manoeuvres, proved too much to handle for a government whose main resort for holding on to authority was a further recurrence of state centralism.

Years after his failed presidential experience Rivadavia became more self-critical about the way in which he had conducted his nation's political affairs, and Bartolomé Mitre claims that he even admitted this by stating that, 'it is necessary to confess that we were

---

5   'Consiste, pues, la principal gloria del señor Rivadavia en haber colocado la moral en la región del poder como base de su fuerza y permanencia, y en comprender que la educación del pueblo es el elemento primordial de la felicidad y engrandecimiento. Sobre estas columnas fundó una administración que todavía no conoce rival en estos países, y parte de cuyas creaciones, como puntos luminosos, han lucido hasta en las negras horas del gobierno bárbaro que por tantos años mantuvo detenido el carro del progreso argentino.' In Gutiérrez, *Bernardino Rivadavia*, pp. 51–2.

ignorants when we attempted to form the Republic in our country'.[6] However, we should always recognise that Rivadavia was the main instigator of the *felíz experiencia* of 1821–24, which in many ways marks the genesis of Argentine cultural life.

6   '[…] es necesario confesar que éramos unos ignorantes, cuando ensayamos constituir la República en nuestro país'. Quoted in *Páginas de un estadista*, p. 216.

INSTITUTE FOR THE STUDY OF THE
A M E R I C A S

The Institute for the Study of the Americas (ISA) promotes, coordinates and provides a focus for research and postgraduate teaching on the Americas — Canada, the USA, Latin America and the Caribbean — in the University of London.

The Institute was officially established in August 2004 as a result of a merger between the Institute of Latin American Studies and the Institute of United States Studies, both of which were formed in 1965.

The Institute publishes in the disciplines of history, politics, economics, sociology, anthropology, geography and environment, development, culture and literature, and on the countries and regions of Latin America, the United States, Canada and the Caribbean.

ISA runs an active programme of events — conferences, seminars, lectures and workshops — in order to facilitate national research on the Americas in the humanities and social sciences. It also offers a range of taught master's and research degrees, allowing wide-ranging multi-disciplinary, multi-country study or a focus on disciplines such as politics or globalisation and development for specific countries or regions.

Full details about the Institute's publications, events, postgraduate courses and other activities are available on the web at *www.americas.sas.ac.uk*.

Institute for the Study of the Americas
School of Advanced Study, University of London
31 Tavistock Square, London WC1H 9HA

Tel 020 7862 8870, Fax 020 7862 8886
Email americas@sas.ac.uk
Web www.americas.sas.ac.uk

Recent and forthcoming titles in the ISA series: